BADMINTON
ESSENTIALS

Tariq Wadood

Total Health Publications
Oslo, Norway
Copyright 2018

About the Author--Tariq Wadood

National Singles and Mixed Doubles Champion Coach, National Men's and Women's Teams Pro, Manhattan Beach Badminton Club, Manhattan Beach, CA

Tariq Wadood is one of the outstanding badminton players and coaches of our time. Before coming to the United States to further his education, he was ranked among the ten top players in the world. He was the national singles champion for nine years and the national doubles champion for ten years in his native Pakistan. He has also taught and coached in Pakistan. After coming to the United States to obtain his Master's degree in mechanical engineering at California State University at Northridge, he began to compete in America. He is currently the national men's and mixed doubles champion in the U.S.A. He is also the coach of the National Men's and Women's teams, and is currently the chief instructor at the Manhattan Beach Badminton Club in California.

Foreword

In my opinion, Tariq Wadood is one of the smoothest badminton players I have ever seen in action. This, of course, is a sign of countless hours of practice, plus a natural athletic ability which allows him to catch on quickly and execute strokes in an apparently effortless manner. For many years this has made Tariq one of the top badminton players in the world.

The combination of Tariq's skill and knowledge as a player and coach, has produced an outstanding textbook on badminton. The many step-by-step photographs of our junior champions in action, in addition to concise drawings of court targets and shuttle trajectories combine to give an easy-to-read, yet comprehensive guide to playing badminton.

Those persons who study the fundamentals and strategies advocated by Tariq will find that their games will improve considerably. So onward to playing and enjoying this great game.

Raymond G. Scott
Former Executive Director
United States Badminton Association

Preface

Badminton has long had stature as a major sport in much of the world. Today, with badminton being not only an Olympic sport but also an NCAA sport, its popularity is rising rapidly in this country. With the rapid increase in the popularity of the sport we felt that it was necessary to develop a book which will allow everyone to learn the sport correctly and to enjoy it more.

The author has worked diligently to give you the basics in every area—from the rules and courtesies of the game to the strokes and strategies. The book allows the player to progress from beginning, to intermediate, and to the advanced levels of play.

The publishers have spared no expense in allowing us to show every aspect of the game in photographs, drawings, and videos-- so that you readers can get the most from our presentation. We have not only explained the details of the game but we have emphasized them in various checklists in each chapter. These checklists will help you to follow a skill simply so that you can do it correctly even if you are a beginning level player.

We hope that you will enjoy reading the book and playing the game as much as we have enjoyed writing it for you. Have fun!

PLEASE NOTE:
To access the videos you must be connected to the internet. E-book readers merely click the link address. Print book readers must write the link address into the address bar of your digital device.

Table of Contents

Foreword 3

Preface 3

CHAPTER 1 8

Introduction To Badminton 8
- Benefits of Playing Badminton 9
- History of Badminton 10
- Checklist on the Basics of the Game 12

CHAPTER 2 13

Equipment and Facilities 13
- The Racket 13
- The Shuttlecock 15
- Clothing 15
- Shoes 16
- Socks 16
- Sweatbands 16
- The Court 17
- Summary 19

CHAPTER 3 20

Laws and Courtesies 20

of the Game 20
- Courtesies 20

Simplified Laws (Rules) of Badminton 22
- The Serve 24

CHAPTER 4 27

Grips, Footwork, and 27

the Ready Position 27
- Grips 27
  - Backhand Grip 29
  - Frying-Pan Grip 29
  - Checklist for the Forehand Grip 30
  - Checklist for the Backhand Grip 30
- The Ready Position 31
  - Home Base for Singles Games 32
  - Footwork 34

CHAPTER 5 38

Service and Service Return 38
- The Serve 38
  - High, Deep Serve 39
  - Short Serve 41
  - Drive Serve 44
  - Backhand Serve 44
- Service Return 46
  - Singles Returns 46
  - Doubles Returns 48
  - Serving and Scoring 51

CHAPTER 6 54

Overhead Strokes 54
- Forehand Overhead Clear 55
- Backhand Overhead Clear 58
- Smash 60
  - Half-Smash 63
  - Drop Shot 64
- Push or Dab Shot 66
- **Forehand Drive** 66
  - Round-the-Head Shot 68

CHAPTER 7 71

Underhand Strokes and Smash Returns 71
- Forehand Underhand Clear 72
  - Backhand Underhand Clear 73
- Underhand Drop 74

  Defensing the Smash 74

https://vimeo.com/288044873/69f24945a7 78

CHAPTER 8 79

Strategy 79

 Basic Strategy 80
  Your Fundamental Shots 80
  Developing Game Strategy During Warm-Up 81
 Singles Strategy 82
  Singles Serving 82
  Return of Service for Singles 82
 Doubles Strategy 85
  Doubles Serving 85
  Return of Service for Doubles 85
   Defensive Strategy for Doubles 86
  Offensive Strategy for Doubles 89
   Combination Strategy 92
   Mixed Doubles Strategy 93
   Mixed Doubles Serving 94
   Return of Service for Mixed Doubles 94

https://vimeo.com/288044741/93b0ea7b32 97

CHAPTER 9 98

Drills 98

APPENDIX A 104

The LAWS of Badminton 104

Badminton Terms 118

CHAPTER 1
Introduction To Badminton

Watch the author (in black shorts) in All England Master's doubles championships/ Click https://vimeo.com/288044889/ff36b5a754

This will give you an idea of the speed of the game at the championship level. You will also see all of the shots that will be explained in the book.

Outline

Benefits of Playing Badminton History of Badminton

Where to Play Badminton

Checklist on the Basics of the Game

Summary

Badminton is a game in which two players (singles game) or four players (doubles game) hit a light, feathered object (shuttlecock) over a net with their rackets. The objective is to win the game of 15 points

(11 points for ladies singles) by hitting the shuttle into the opponent's court and preventing it from landing within the boundaries of your own court.

The strategy of winning involves using a variety of shots to force your opponent to lose the rally. The players attempt to move their opponents around the court, forcing weak returns, or they hit hard shots (smashes) that the opponents cannot return.

Benefits of Playing Badminton

A major benefit of badminton is that it is so easy to learn that it is fun almost as soon as you pick up your racket for the first time. Yet, as your skill level increases, the game involves much more strategy and demands greater physical conditioning. Therefore, your enjoyment of the game should increase as your skill level develops. For these reasons it is one of the most popular sports internationally. At the advanced level it is the fastest court game in the world.

Badminton is also a very social sport. It produces a congenial atmosphere that encourages easy interaction among people of both sexes in both school and club environments. Since the game can be played indoors or outdoors, and its court is relatively small (20 x 44 feet), badminton can be played almost anywhere. This makes it a fine family recreation.

There are obvious physical benefits to the game. The long rallies aid in the development of cardiovascular fitness. The stretching and twisting also aid in developing flexibility. The nature of the game develops an increased level of agility and coordination.

On a psychological level badminton helps reduce tensions as players move around the court and strike the shuttle. Additionally, as they improve in skill, they develop a higher level of self-satisfaction that comes with the accomplishment of any goal.

Badminton, as we know it today, is second only to soccer as the world's most popular participation activity. An activity for all ages and for both sexes, it is a unique and exciting competitive sport. When the shuttle is hit by a skilled player, it can reach a speed well over 200 miles per hour or float delicately over the net. No other sport has as great a variation of speed.

Because of the limited exposure badminton receives in the United States, many people hold the erroneous belief that it is not a vigorous and challenging activity. When observing beginners hitting the shuttle slowly over the net, it becomes easy to draw this conclusion. But given the proper instruction, the players can learn to control the tempo of the game, and it becomes fascinating to watch as well as to play. As the players learn more strokes, the rallies become more exciting.

Many racket sports are difficult and frustrating to learn. In badminton, even beginning players can start a rally almost immediately and gain a sense of achievement. Whether you are playing just for the exercise or planning to enter competition, it is an excellent cardiovascular activity. It requires fast reflexes, good physical conditioning, and concentration.

Furthermore, badminton is a "lifetime sport," not just one for the young.

History of Badminton

While there is some evidence that a game similar to badminton (called *battledore)* was played in China 2,000 years ago, badminton as it is presently played originated in England. The English royal court records refer to a similar sport as early as the twelfth century. Most historians believe that English officers brought the game they called *Poona* to India in the seventeenth century. They then brought it back home again to England in the late nineteenth century. In 1873 they played Poona at the Duke of Beaufort's estate, called Badminton House, near the village of Badminton in Gloucestershire, England. The name of the Duke's estate soon became the name of the game. It was from this time that the game began to develop rapidly as a popular pastime.

The first badminton club was formed in Bath, England, in 1873. The game was introduced to North America in the 1890s. In 1895 the National Badminton Association of America was formed, and in 1899 the first All England championship tournament for men was played. The next year the championship for women was inaugurated.

As the sport gained in popularity, it became necessary to establish the rules, equipment, and court dimensions. Eventually, in 1893 the English Badminton Association was organized to bring some uniformity in competition. The rules, called laws, have changed little since this time period.

In 1909, the shuttle that we use today was introduced. Prior to this time very fast and unpredictable *missiles* made with poultry feathers arbitrarily stuck into a piece of cork were used. The court was originally shaped like a wasp or hourglass. Today the court is rectangular, and the tournament shuttles are made of very uniform goose feathers inserted into a precisely shaped cork base. In earlier days, the racket was heavy, but modern technology has produced a dramatic change in weight.

Since 1929 badminton has increased in popularity in the United States. The game is played in clubs and in competition between high schools and colleges across the country. It will become a full Olympic medal sport starting in 1992. Some colleges are giving athletic scholarships for badminton because it will soon be a National Collegiate Athletic Association (NCAA) sport.

There are many local and national tournaments and a world championship for individuals. In addition, national teams compete for the Thomas Cup (similar to the Davis Cup in tennis) for men and the Uber Cup for women. Three singles matches and two doubles matches decide the winner in each competition.

Checklist on the Basics of the Game

1. Most games are completed with 23 points.
2. Either side can score on any rally.
3. During a rally the players attempt to get their opponents to miss a shot by forcing them out of position or hitting a hard shot that cannot be returned.

Summary

1. Badminton as we know it originated in England.
2. It is a sport that can be enjoyed at any age—a "lifetime sport.
3. Badminton can be as slow and relaxing or as vigorous and taxing as you want it to be.
4. The game requires speed, finesse, cardiovascular endurance, and strength.

CHAPTER 2
Equipment and Facilities

Outline

The Racket

The Shuttlecock

Sweatbands
The Court
Checklist for Game or
Practice Equipment
Summary

The Racket

The racket is very light so that it can be moved quickly with a flick of the wrist. It may be made of wood, metal, or synthetic material such as graphite, boron, carbon or ceramic. Beginners do not need an expensive racket, but advanced players may look for special features and special weights that may bring the cost from $40 to $150.

The metal and synthetic rackets are generally stronger and lighter. Because of their strength, they do not need to be placed in a press to retain their shape as the wood rackets require. They can also be strung tighter (17 to 22 pounds) so that the shuttle will fly farther when hit.

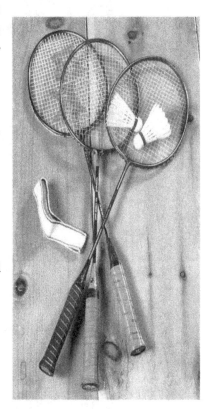

The type of game one plays determines the type of racket one should choose. If you enter into competitive badminton you will soon decide whether to be primarily an offensive or a defensive player. An offensive player hits hard and tries to score points that way. A defensive player tries to return every shot back and force the opponent into making mistakes. Every player must have both offensive and defensive skills, but most advanced players will emphasize one style or the other.

Offensive-minded players generally use rackets more heavily weighted in the head. This gives the player more potential power in a shot. Defensive players use light-headed rackets.

The head, or *face,* of the racket is strung with strings of gut, nylon, or a similar material. Nylon string usually costs less and lasts longer. Tournament players usually use gut, however, because it can be strung with more tension so that the shuttle will bounce from it with more speed.

The *grip* is the part of the handle that is covered with leather or composition. Most companies make only two sizes of grip. Some make three. (The range in circumference is from $3^1/_4$ to 3 Vs inches.) The grip should be sufficiently large so that your hand comfortably wraps around it and you feel that it is in no danger of slipping as you hit the shuttlecock.

The Shuttlecock

The *shuttlecock,* usually called the *shuttle* or *bird,* weighs about one-sixth of an ounce (more technically about 4 grams or 73 to 85 grains). The official shuttles are made of goose feathers placed in a cork head that is leather-covered. This is the type of shuttle used in all high-level play. Beginners and school classes often use a cheaper and more durable plastic or nylon shuttle.

When the temperature is high or you are playing at a higher altitude, the air is thinner. You will then want a lighter shuttle so that it will fall more slowly. Heavier shuttles are used closer to sea level, in climates with a higher humidity, and for outdoor playing.

Clothing

.Shorts and shirts are generally worn by both men and women, although some women wear tennis dresses or skirts. The preferred color is white. It helps disguise the white shuttlecock (seen against the backdrop of white clothing)—especially when a player is serving. While most clubs and tournaments allow the same kinds of clothing worn for tennis, some specify a particular type and color. It is wise to check with the director to determine local requirements.

Shirts are generally made of cotton because it has better perspiration-absorption qualifies than synthetic fabrics. All clothing should allow you to stretch comfortably.

Shoes

Because of the quick starting and stopping involved in badminton, a tennis shoe is preferred. It should have a non-marking sole with nonskid tread. The preferred color of the shoe is white. Do not use jogging shoes, aerobic shoes, or shoes designed for other sports. They will not give you the lateral foot stability that you need for badminton.

Your shoes should be laced from the bottom eyelets. Pull the laces firm at each higher eyelet. This helps to give you a snug fit and prevent the rubbing that can result in blisters.

Socks

The socks should be wool or cotton to absorb perspiration. In order to avoid blisters you may want to wear two pairs of lighter socks. The two socks rub against each other and reduce the friction between the shoe and the skin that might otherwise result in a blister. The socks should be white.

Sweatbands

If you perspire heavily, you might want to wear a sweatband on your forehead. The sweatband not only reduces the perspiration that can run into your eyes, but it also keeps your hair away from your face. Wristbands prevent perspiration from rolling down your arm and getting your hand sweaty, possibly causing your grip to slip.

The Court

The badminton court is 44 feet long. The singles court is 17 feet wide, while the doubles court is 20 feet wide. The lines are inbounds. The top of the net is 5 feet, 1 inch, at the post and 5 feet at the center of the court.

There is a short service line 6 feet, 6 inches, from the net. The server must stand behind this line, in the service court area, and the serve must clear the opposite short service line to be in play.

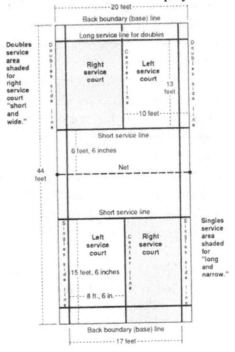

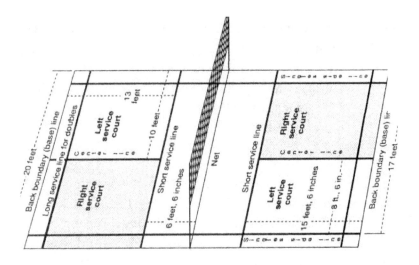

The serving court for singles is bounded by the short service line, the centerline, the singles sideline, and the back boundary of the court. This produces a long, narrow court 15 feet, 6 inches, long and 8 feet, 6 inches, wide. The server must stand within this court and serve into the diagonally opposite singles court in order to have a legal serve.

The doubles service court is shorter but wider than the singles court. It is bounded by the short service line in front, the centerline, the doubles sideline, and a line 2 feet, 6 inches, in from the rear boundary. The doubles server must stand in this court and serve to the diagonally opposite doubles court to begin play.

There should be at least 20 feet of clearance overhead-24 to 30 feet is considered ideal. A 30-foot ceiling is required for national and international competition.

Checklist for Being Ready to Play

    a. One or two rackets.
    b. Two tubes of shuttlecocks. .

    c. Shoes and socks.
    d. Towel.
    e. Sweatbands for forehead and wrist (optional).
    f. Shirt and shorts.

Summary

1. Rackets can be made of wood, metal, or other materials.

2. Offensive players generally use a racket heavier in the head than the racket defensive players would choose.

3. The shuttlecock can be made of feathers and cork or plastic. The plastic or nylon shuttle plays longer, but the feathers give a better flight and a steeper drop.

4. Clothing should be comfortable enough to allow you to run unimpaired and to stretch easily. The preferred color is white.

5. Shoes should be tennis or all-court shoes with a good nonskid sole.

CHAPTER 3
Laws and Courtesies of the Game

Outline
Courtesies
Simplified Laws (Rules) of Badminton

Courtesies

The game of badminton emphasizes good sportsmanship, expressed through certain playing *courtesies.* It is expected that you will be friendly to and respectful of your opponent, and gracious whether winning or losing. In addition, here are some specific courtesies expected from those who play badminton.

1. Introduce yourself to your partner and to your opponents before the match. Be sure to shake hands after the match.
2. While warming up, help your opponent's warm-up as well; don't kill every stroke.
3. If there is any question on whether or not you have fouled, call it on yourself.
4. When you are in doubt about whether a shuttle landed in or out, always give the benefit of the doubt to your opponent or replay the point.
5. Never question your opponent's calls.
6. While there are times during a match in which you may want to aim a smash at your opponent, do not do it if you can get the point any other way. If you have a set-up, hit it somewhere else in the court.
7. Control your anger. Never throw your racket.
8. Never deride or make fun of an opponent.
9. As the server, keep the score and call it before each serve—calling the server's score first.
10. When your opponent is serving and a shuttle lands on your side of the court, pick it up and hit it back, or toss it under the net to the server.
11. Compliment your opponent on any good shots made.
12. Do not offer advice or criticism to your partner or your opponents.
13. Bring your share of shuttlecocks to every practice and game.
14. Keep up the play. Do not stall between points.
15. Do not talk to your partner during a rally except when you are directing tactics, as in, "I've got it," or "You're up."

16. If you are receiving, be ready to return the shuttle as soon as the server is ready to serve.

Simplified Laws (Rules) of Badminton

The complete laws of the game will be found in Appendix A of this book. A summary follows:

1. Toss for the serve. You can flip a coin, spin a racket, or toss a shuttle to determine who gets the choice of "side or serve." If spinning a racket, identify a marking on the racket then spin it in the hand or on the floor. One person calls the mark. If it is called correctly that person gets the choice. The most common method of determining the choice, however, is by hitting or tossing the shuttle into the air and letting it land. The person towards whom the base of the shuttle is pointing gets the choice. If the winner of the toss chooses a side of the court to defend, the other person can choose to serve or receive.

The side of the court may become important if one side has poorer lighting or an undesirable background. In an important match the player who wins the toss might elect to defend the less desirable side first. This would then have him or her on the best side for the last half of the third game.

2. Games (singles and doubles) are played to 21 points with rally scoring—either team can score

on any rally. The old rules allowed only the server to score.

The game should be won by 2 points so if it is 20 all, the first person to be two points ahead wins. The exception is if the game goes to 29 all—The next point will win.

3. The serve, if not played by the receiver, must land in the diagonal service court. Any shuttle hitting the line is in. In singles the shuttle must land in the long, narrow court. In doubles it must land in the short, wide court. In doubles the long service line is for the service boundary only. Once the serve has been hit, the full court (20 x 44 feet) is played.

The serve is made from the right service court whenever the server's score is an even number (0, 2, 4, etc.). The serve is from the left court whenever the server's score is an odd number (1, 3, 5, etc.)

When the receiving side has won a point, it gains the serve.

In doubles the order of serving is:

Initial server from right service court. When the receiving side wins a point, the partner of the initial receiver serves. When that serving team loses the serve the partner of the initial server serves. When the serving team loses the point, the initial receiver will serve. When that team loses its serve, the initial server will serve again. This order of service continues through the game.

In doubles the server serves until the serving team commits a fault, and the serve is lost.

4. Most matches are "best two out of three games." The winner of the match will be the one who wins two games. The players will change sides of the court after each game—and in the third game when the first player has reached 11 points.

The Serve

When serving the whole shuttlecock must be below the waist and the racket must be pointing downward.

Correct serve

Shuttlecock above the waist and racket shaft not pointing down.

The server has only one chance to serve.

Incorrect serve

Faults (loss of serve for the serving team or loss of the point for the receiving team) occur whenever

A serve is illegal for the following reasons:

1. The shuttle is hit when it is above the waist.
2. The head of the racket is above the hand when the shuttle is hit.
3. The server misses the shuttle when trying to hit it.
4. Any serve or other shot does one of the following:

24

- Goes under or through the net.
- Hits an overhead obstruction.
- Hits a player inside or outside of the court.

- A serve lands outside the proper service area.
- A shot lands out of bounds (only if the head, not the feathers of the shuttle lands outside the lines).
- Either the server or receiver steps out of the proper court before the shuttle is served.
- The receiving player does not play the shuttle. (Only the proper receiver may return the serve.)

- A player reaches over the net to hit the shuttle. (It is legal to follow through over the net provided that the player or racket does not hit the net.)
- A player touches the net with the racket or any part of the body or clothing. A player hits the shuttle twice (a *double hit*) or carries it on the racket (rather than having it bounce

quickly from the strings) before it crosses the net.
- The server steps forward when serving.
- A player obstructs or hinders an opponent.
- A player catches the shuttle and calls it *out*.

Summary

1. Badminton is a game in which good sportsmanship is expected.
2. The courtesies spell out the expected behavior of a badminton player.
3. The shuttle cannot be double-hit.
4. The lines are in.

CHAPTER 4
Grips, Footwork, and the Ready Position

Outline

Grips
Forehand Grip
Backhand Grip
Flying-Pan Grip
Checklist for the Forehand Grip
Checklist for the Backhand Grip
The Ready Position
Ready Position for Return of Service
Home Base for Singles Games Checklist for Ready Position Footwork
Summary

Grips

The basics of badminton skills start with the grip. Without the proper grip you will not be able to execute strokes effectively or efficiently. There are two essential grips—the forehand and the backhand. The following description is for right-handed players. If you are left-handed just reverse the instructions. Remember that whichever grip you use, you should check it often to make sure it is correct.

Forehand Grip

Hold the head of your racket perpendicular to the floor and "shake hands" with the grip on the handle of the racket. There will be a "V" formed by the juncture of your thumb and index finger. It should be slightly left of center on the top of the grip. The grip should be with your fingers, not the palm of your hand. Your fingers should be slightly spread, with your forefinger extended even farther out. The grip is different from the way you would grip a hammer.

Your thumb wraps around the handle and rests on the side of the middle finger. The palm of the hand should be parallel with the face of the racket. The butt of the racket handle should be touching the heel of your hand.

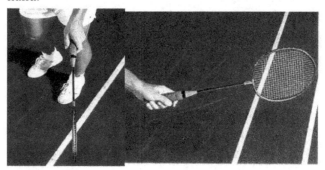

Forehand grip—   left hander

The grip should be rather loose. A tight grip will cause tension in your hand and wrist. As you hit a shot, you will tighten your fingers.

Backhand Grip

There are two types of backhand grips. The first has the racket moved a quarter-turn clockwise (so that as your thumb moves farther behind the racket, the back of your hand moves toward the top of the handle). The knuckle of your index finger will now be on the top of the handle, and your thumb will be behind the handle, pointing up the shaft. The "V" formed at the base of your thumb and index finger will now be over the top bevel of the handle.

For strokes taken on the backhand (non-racket) side of the body, the grip must be changed to a backhand grip. Otherwise, the racket face will point slightly upward and you will not have control of the shot.

Some players believe that they have more power with this technique. The disadvantage is for shots behind you. In this case the grip loses some of its effectiveness. This is also the grip used in the backhand serve.

The second type of backhand grip changes only the position of the thumb from the forehand grip. It moves from behind the handle to a position along the upper left corner of it. This grip is more efficient for shots behind you. Some players prefer it for other shots as well.

Frying-Pan Grip

Sometimes used by more advanced players, the so-called frying-pan grip is used primarily in doubles play at the net and for service returns. To get the feel of this grip, place the racket on the floor and grasp it like a frying pan, about an inch above the end of the handle. This is also known as the western grip.

Checklist for the Forehand Grip

1. With the racket head perpendicular to the floor, is the "V" formed by the thumb and index finger on top of the handle grip?
2. Is the index finger separated from the middle finger by resting higher on the handle?
3. Is the grip loose rather than tight?
4. Is the racket held in the fingers rather than in the palm of your hand?

Checklist for the Backhand Grip

1. Did you move your hand a quarter-turn toward the back side of the handle?
2. Is the first knuckle of the index finger on top of the handle?
3. Is your thumb behind the handle and pointing up the shaft?

The Ready Position

Rally Ready

The rally-ready position is taken whenever you are ready to hit a shot, whether it be a smash, a drive, or a drop. From this position you will be best able to move effectively forward or back and right or left. It is similar to the "ready position" for most sports. Your feet should be spread to shoulder width or slightly wider. Your ankles and knees should be slightly flexed, and you should be bent forward at the waist. Your weight should be slightly on the balls of your feet so that you are ready to move in any direction. (If you curl your toes down just a bit, you will feel your weight on the forward part of your feet.)

Your arms should be forward, with the racket-holding hand at about waist height—ready to move to a forehand or backhand hit. And you should be relaxed, because you can move more quickly when you are relaxed than when you are tense.

Ready Position for Return of Service

This position is slightly different. You will keep your non-racket foot (left foot for right-handers) forward. This will allow you to move more quickly up and back as necessary to return a service. The racket head will be in front of your right shoulder for right-handers or the left shoulder for left-handers.

If the serve is behind you, push off your left foot, and run or shuffle back to the spot where you will hit the shuttle. If the serve is hit short, bring your right foot forward and attack the shuttle.

Home Base for Singles Games

In badminton you do not have time to get ready for most shots as you do in tennis or golf. For this reason you must *always* be ready to react to the shuttle. The best position from which to defend your court is in the middle of the court—on the centerline, a few feet ahead of a spot halfway between the net and the back boundary line. (This puts you about 2 feet behind the "T" that is formed by the centerline meeting the front service line.) From this position you can get to the front court to handle the drop shots and will still have time to move back to play the clears.

Depending on your individual strength and quickness, you might want to play a few feet ahead or behind this center area. Your home-base position may also vary depending on your opponent. You might play farther forward if the opponent is weaker or uses a lot of drop shots. You might play farther back against a strong smasher or clearing player.

As you become more advanced, you may move a bit to one side or the other to take away your opponent's angle of return. When you hit to a deep corner, your opponent has a greater angle in which to return to your court. If you hit to the center of the court, the angle is reduced.

Always try to get to home base after every shot. However, if your opponent is ready to hit the shuttle and you haven't yet returned to your home base, stop and get set to defend your court from wherever you are on the court.

Footwork

Good footwork is essential in badminton. You must be able to get to the shuttle quickly before you can hit your stroke. Being a little slow getting into position will force you to make a less effective shot. For example, not being behind a smash will greatly reduce the downward angle of the shot and may make the shuttle go too high or too long.

From your ready position you should be able to move quickly as your opponent hits the shuttle. Watch  the shuttle as it leaves your opponent's racket, and push off hard with the foot that is away from where you want to move—your left foot if you are moving to the right. Keep your feet low to the ground to avoid wasted motion.

For deep shots get your body turned sideways so that your chest is facing the sideline near the shuttle. For shots close to the net, your final step will be with your racket side foot (right foot for right-handers).

The best way to improve footwork is *shadow practice.* Simply have someone on the other side of the net point to a spot where the imaginary shuttle is flying. Move quickly to that position and swing as if you were hitting the shuttle. Quickly return to the base position, in the center of the court, after each shot.

For shots hit close to the net, remember that you will always hit the shot with your racket-side foot closest to the point of contact. (Right foot for right-handers.) If the shuttle is a long way away, step with the left foot first, then with the right foot. If it is close, just step with the right foot.

For shots deep in the court, the more advanced players will scissor their legs as they hit. The right foot may be back while the backswing is being completed, but the player will jump and hit, switching the legs and gaining ground back toward the base position.

Warm up

As in any physical sport, badminton players must prepare their bodies for the rigors of the game. The warm-up should include stretching and moving your muscles so that you will be able to move quickly when the game starts. A proper warm-up also helps avoid injuries to muscles and joints during the game. Some guidelines follow:

- Jog around the gym, or do relaxed jumping jacks for a minute. This warms up your muscles and allows your body to stretch more efficiently.
- Swing your arms in big circles forward and back—ten times each.

- With your feet spread, reach up high with your right arm, then twist your whole body right then immediately turn to the left.
- Begin a slow rally to warm up while playing. You can start your rally while jumping up and down (as if you were rope jumping). This helps your legs get ready for the more forceful contractions you will have to make in the game.
- Take your racket and practice imaginary shots—first slowly then faster.
- Rally with a partner.

Cooling Down

After you have played, don't just shake hands and sit down, or your muscles will tighten. A cool-down reduces later muscle soreness and helps eliminate the build-up of waste products (such as lactic acid) in your body. Take a short walk, or do some of the stretches that you did for your warm-up. The idea is to allow your muscles to gradually relax and cool down.

Summary

The grip is very important. Without the proper grip for the chosen stroke, you will drastically reduce your chances of making an effective shot.

1. The ready position is similar to that used in many other sports. It should allow the player to move quickly in any direction.
2. Always have your racket up and ready so that you can take the offense.
3. The home-base position is in midcourt and slightly forward of the midpoint of the centerline.
4. Good footwork is essential in badminton.
5. Always warm up adequately for your rally or game.
6. Cool down after the game to reduce the chance of muscle soreness.

CHAPTER 5
Service and Service Return

Outline

The Serve

High, Deep Serve

Checklist for High Deep

Checklist for Low, Backhand Serve

Service Return

Singles Returns

Doubles Returns

The Serve

The serve should be learned first, since all rallies start with one. Also, it is through the serve that a player begins to "control the point."

The rules state that, when serving, you must stand in the service court, and your feet must both stay in contact with the floor until after the shuttle is hit. During your arm action, your racket must contact the shuttle below your waist, and the entire head of your racket must be below your hand.

High, Deep Serve

The high, deep service is used primarily in singles play. If not hit by your opponent, this serve should land as close as possible to his or her opponent's back line. The objective is to move your opponent deep into the back court.

Take a position approximately 2 to 3 feet from the front service line and close to the centerline. (The point where the center line meets the front service line is often called the "T.") Stand with your feet comfortably apart (about shoulder width), with your racket-side foot back (the right foot for right-handed players). Your knees should be slightly bent.

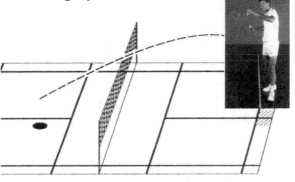

Hold the shuttle by its cork base between the thumb and the index and middle finger of your left hand. Extend your left arm outward in front of the right shoulder. This allows you to hit the shuttle near waist level and in front of you. Many beginners tend to hold the shuttle low, near waist level, then drop it. This forces them to hit it at too low a point. You always want to hit the shuttle at as high a point as is legally possible.

39

Your right wrist will be cocked up and back so that the racket head will be raised and the wrist will be at or above waist level. Your weight will be on your rear (right) foot.

As you drop the shuttle in front and to the side of your body (at about 45-degree angle), your weight will shift forward (to your left foot), and you will swing the racket through the shuttle. At the contact point, the entire head of the racket must be below the level of your hand and below waist level.

Your body rotates in the direction of the shuttle's flight, and your wrist straightens and snaps the racket through the shuttle. You should be hitting up and out.

Follow through over your left shoulder, and let your forearm continue its rotation. Remember that you are not allowed to move or slide either foot until after contact is made with the shuttle.

The only difference in your stance between serving from the right and left courts is that when you are serving from the left, your back foot will be further behind your front foot.

The most common error for beginners is bringing the racket forward before dropping the shuttle. This results in missing it completely—a fault.

Since the shuttlecock is very light and is designed to catch a great deal of air in its flight, it drops slowly. Your racket swing must compensate for this slow drop. So the idea is to drop the shuttle, then hit it after it is already dropping.

Checklist for High Deep Serve

1. Do I have a forehand grip?

2. Is my non-racket hand extended outward to where the shuttle can be dropped effectively?

3. Is my racket behind my body with the wrist cocked?

4. Did I drop the shuttle before I started the racket forward?

5. Was the shuttle dropped to the racket side of my body?

6. Did I contact the shuttle at about knee height?

7. Did I bring the racket through quickly by using the power of my wrist and forearm?

8. Did I follow through over my non-racket shoulder?

Did I hit the shuttle up and out?

Short Serve

The low, short serve is used more often in doubles than in singles. The doubles service court is not as long as the singles service court, so the high, clear serves cannot be hit deeply. But since the doubles service court is wider than the singles court, the short serves can be placed farther from the receiver. In addition, the low serve forces your opponent to hit the shuttle up and gives you the opportunity to take the offensive by hitting the shuttle down.

It takes a great deal of practice to be able to serve the shuttle low over the net and to land it close to the front corners of your opponent's service court. When used in singles it can keep your opponent off balance or bring him or her closer to the net so that the deep serves will be more effective.

Take a position about 2 to 3 feet from the front service line and close to the centerline. Both arms will stay close to your body while your weight rests on your forward foot.

Right hander

Left hander

Drop the shuttle before you start your racket forward. Your wrist will be cocked backward and upward. It will stay cocked throughout the stroke—even during the follow-through. Drop the shuttle in front of, and to the side of, your body, and swing the racket in a nearly horizontal plane around your body—with the racket head just below waist level. The racket head should be angled slightly upward to direct the shuttle just over the net. Gently guide the shuttle forward so that it just clears the net. Beginners should clear the net by 12 inches or less, advanced players by no more than

2 inches. The serve should then fall into your opponent's service area just past the service line. lithe shuttle touches the net but still falls into the correct service court, it is a legal serve. The short serves should fall just past the service line. Try to hit either of the front corners of the opponent's service court. The short serve requires a great deal of practice.

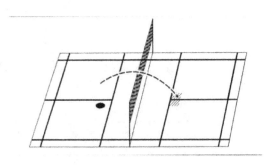

1) Do I have a forehand grip?
2) Is most of my weight on my forward foot?
3) Are my elbows bent and close to my waist?
4) Is my right hand near my right hip?

5) Is my wrist cocked backwards?
6) Did I drop the shuttle before I started my racket swing?
7) Was the shuttle dropped to the front and right side of my body?
8) At contact did my wrist remain cocked?
9) Did I guide the shuttle over the net with my right forearm?

Flick Serve

The *flick serve* is a harder-hit serve with a low trajectory, just high enough to clear the outstretched racket when your opponent is reaching up to return it. It is used in both singles and doubles—most often in doubles, when your opponent often rushes your short serve.

The shuttle is dropped in front and away from the body. The flick serve should look just like a short serve, except that as the racket nears the shuttle, its speed is accelerated to drive the shuttle to the back court by uncocking the wrist. If the serve is not returned, it should land deep in your opponent's back court.

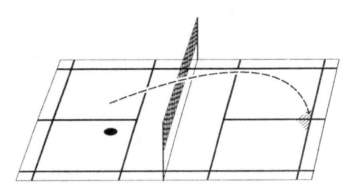

Drive Serve

The *drive serve* is hit hard, but lower than a flick serve. It is used more often in doubles, when your opponent is expecting a short serve. Doubles teams that play a side-by-side alignment may find it especially valuable because it can force a weak return. Beginners may occasionally use this serve in singles, but advanced players do not, because it is easy for the advanced opponent to reach and cut it off.

Backhand Serve

The *backhand serve* is used in doubles as a more effective method of serving the low short serve. It was developed in Indonesia in the 1960s and is now becoming popular in the western countries. In this serve there is very little backswing, and the shuttlecock is hit just after it leaves the hand. Consequently, it takes less time to clear the net, giving your opponent less time to adjust to your serve. Also, because the white shuttle blends in with the white clothing of the player, it is more difficult for the receiver to see.

For this serve your stance will be parallel to the net. (When your shoulders and an imaginary line touching the front of the toes on each of your feet are parallel to the net, your stance is parallel. Some players will only have their

racket-side foot forward.) Your grip will be the true backhand grip, with your thumb behind the racket handle.

Thumb and index finger should lightly grip just one or two feathers of the shuttle, holding it just below your waist and parallel to the face of the racket. (Some people like the racket face perpendicular to the floor; others like the face opened toward the ceiling. Whichever racket position you choose, the shuttle should be parallel to the racket face.)

Your right elbow will be shoulder-high, and your right arm will be away from your body. Your forearm and racket extend at a 45-degree angle downward. Remember that the shuttle has to be hit below the waist to be legal. It should just barely clear the net, landing close to your opponent's serve line. For variation, this serve can be hit harder and become a flick or a elear.

Checklist for Low, Backhand Serve

1. Do I have a backhand grip with the thumb behind the handle?
2. Is my grip higher on the handle—away from the base?
3. Is my stance parallel to the net?
4. Am I holding the shuttle below my waist and by the tip of the feathers?
5. Is my racket-arm elbow shoulder-high and away from my body?
6. Is the racket head angled down behind the shuttle?
7. Did I "push" the shuttle over the net?
8. Did the shuttle start dropping before it passed to the other side of the net?

Service Return

Your body position for the service return is as follows: left shoulder and foot forward, feet spread about 2 feet apart, with most of your weight on your forward foot so that you can move backward more quickly, and knees and ankles flexed, with weight on the balls of your feet. Your torso is flexed forward, and your racket is held up above your head and ready to hit.

Singles Returns

Your position on the court will be slightly forward of midcourt and slightly to the backhand side of your service court. To return a singles serve, you would be a bit deeper. From the left court, you will be the same distance back but closer to the center of the service court—the midline between the sideline and the centerline. Your alignment should allow you to protect your backhand so that you have a greater chance of playing the return with a forehand.

Watch the shuttle before it is served, and be alert for any possible serve. Then get to it as quickly as possible in order to catch it at its highest point. Hitting lazy underhand returns puts no pressure on the serving team.

On short serves, quickly lunge forward to the net. Your best choices of a return shot are: (1) a drop to the front corner away from your opponent or (2) a high clear. On the deeper flick serves, jump back quickly, and hit a drop or a smash.

Your best strategy is to place your shot in an area of the court that forces your opponents to play defense. Use high clears to the backhand corners and drops along the net. The most effective types of returns are

- Clear return.
- Attacking clear return.
- Smash or half-smash.
- Drop return.

The *clear return* (also used in doubles) is a high shot that clears the opponent and lands just inside the back line. Keep it away from your opponent, preferably to the backhand side. Make your opponent move. This is especially effective if you have been hitting drop returns, leading your opponent to anticipate another drop and thus come to the net. As with other clearing shots, you will need a strong wrist action and a follow-through along the intended line of flight.

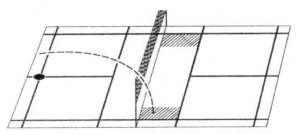

The *attacking clear return* can be used if the opponent has hit a high, weak serve and is close to the net. The trajectory in this return is lower, so the opponent has less time to react to the shot. It is aimed just like the regular clear return. The danger in this return is that if the opponent is quick to react, he or she can cut the shuttle off and smash it.

The *smash* or *half-smash return* can be used when a clear serve is too short or too low. It puts your opponent on the defensive by forcing an upward hit.

The *drop return* can be used anytime you want to move your opponent away from the center position. If your opponent has hit a drop serve, you can counter

A. Right court

B. Left court

with an underhand drop return close to the net.

Doubles Returns

Stand within a foot of the front service line and within a foot of the center service line. This will allow you to attack the low serve quickly and force your opponents to play defense.

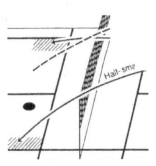

Unless you find it very successful, don't rush to the net on your return too often. While you may occasionally guess correctly that your opponent is hitting a short serve, your opponent may also catch on to your strategy and catch you off-guard with a high serve.

Your return strategy should be to force your opponent deep with a clear, or to hit down so that your opponent must hit up with a defensive shot. The most effective returns are

Short service return attack in doubles

- Drop return.
- Clear return.
- Half-court pushes down the middle or to the sidelines (into the alley).
- Harder pushes or drives down the middle or to the deep corners.

Vary your returns to keep your opponents off-balance.

The *doubles drop return* must be very close to the net and close to the near sideline as it is returned to your opponent. (Unless your opponent is out of position, do not hit this shot crosscourt.) This is because in doubles your opponents will usually play one person up and one back. The person close to the net will therefore have a better chance of smashing it back if it is hit high. Consequently, you have to hit lower and wider in doubles than in singles.

The *halfcourt push return* is a difficult shot because it must be played nearly perfectly or your opponents may gain the advantage. When placed correctly, it will fall low behind the net player and force the back player to hit up. If it is a backhand shot, make certain that your thumb is behind the handle in a good backhand grip.

The ***push return*** is a nearly sidearm return (backhand or forehand) that is pushed with the forearm into the deep backhand corner, deep forehand corner, or into your opponent's body. It starts downward from your racket.

The *doubles drive return* is hit along the sidelines with a short, fast backswing. It is used if your opponents are playing up and back and should always be hit straight down the near sideline.

Contact the shuttle in front of your body and within 2 feet of the net. It is hit flat, with the racket head parallel to the net. Only the wrist is used in this shot.

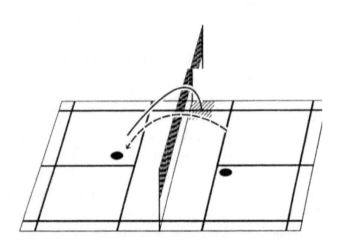

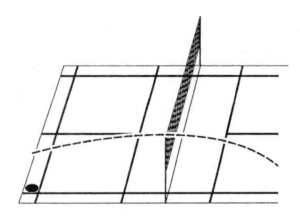

Trajectory for drive return.

The *clear return* is the same as in singles.

Serving and Scoring

In singles the serve is from the right service court whenever the server's score is an even number. The serve is from the left court whenever the server's score is an odd number. Remember that the service court for singles is long and narrow and that the sideline is the inside court boundary.

In doubles the serving team will always start an inning with the server in the right service court serving first. If the serving team wins the point, the same server moves to the left court and serves. The server keeps alternating courts until the serve is lost by a fault. (See Chapter 3.)

When the first server has lost the serve in the first inning of play, the service is over, and the opponents serve. The team that serves first in doubles keeps the serve only as long as the original server continues to make points. (After the very first inning, each player continues to serve until there is a fault.)

The opponents' first server will serve from the right court. If a point is made, he or she will move to the left court. Courts are alternated until the first server has lost the serve. The second server will then serve from the same court in which he or she was standing when the serve was lost. In other words, one cannot serve twice in a row to the same receiver. After the starting team has lost the service, the second team serving is allowed to have each server serve until the point is lost.

Once the original receivers have both lost their serves (called *two hands down)* the team that served first in the game will regain the serve. This time each player on that team must lose his/her serve before the other team gets another turn at serving.

A simple way to remember who should serve first in an inning is to remember which side of the court you were in during your team's first serve. You should be on that same side whenever your team's score is zero or an even number. You should be on the other side of the court whenever your team's score is an odd number.

The *rally* begins once the shuttle is served legally over the net, and it continues until one team has made a fault. If the serving team faults, the partner then takes the turn.

Once you begin to play, you will realize the importance of position, footwork, and strategy.

Summary

1. Only the person serving can score points, so the serve is very important.

2. The basic serves are the clear and the short, but a flick serve or a backhand serve can also be used. In singles the high, deep serve is most often used; in doubles, the low, short serve. The drive serve is a change-up serve that can be very effective as is the flick serve.

3. Whether playing singles or doubles, mix up your serves.

4. In singles the server serves from the right court whenever the server's score is an even number-0, 2, 4, etc. The server serves from the left

court whenever the score is an odd number-1, 3, 5, etc.

    5.   In doubles the first inning allows only one player to serve. That player serves first from the right court and alternates sides with each point won. When the other team gains its serve, the server in the right court serves until his or her team has committed a fault. Then the partner serves. After each point the server alternates courts.

> Notice doubles serves and returns in this championship, with the author (in black shorts) Click:
>
> https://vimeo.com/288044889/ff36b5a754

CHAPTER 6
Overhead Strokes

The overhead strokes that are absolutely essential for any badminton player are the clear, the smash and half-smash, drop, dab or push, and the drive.

These are the "fun" strokes. There are very few service aces in badminton. Most of the points come from rallies. Since the net is 5 feet high, you will want to hit most strokes above your head. This way you have the option of hitting downward hard or hitting a controlling shot that places the shuttle quickly in an area difficult for your opponent to cover.

If you are forced to hit underhand, your choices are limited, allowing your opponent to control the game. To be in control, you must play an attacking game by hitting as many overhead shots as possible, forcing your opponent to hit up or to hit from deep in the backcourt.

The fundamental overhead strokes for beginners are:
- Forehand and backhand clears and drops.
- Forehand smash.

The intermediate-level overhead shots are
- Drives.
- Round-the-head shots.

The advanced overhead shots are
- Backhand smash.
- Attacking clear.
- Half-smash.

Forehand Overhead Clear

The *forehand overhead clear* is used mostly in singles to move an opponent to the back court. Take a forehand grip; then, from your base position, watch the oncoming shuttle and get into position behind it, with your right shoulder in line with it. Bring your racket up and behind your shoulders with the racket head pointing slightly downward. This is often called the *back-scratching* position because the racket head is nearly touching your back. Get into this position quickly. If you

hit the shuttle while you are moving backwards, you are not getting back and behind the shuttle quickly enough.

When you hit this shot, your left shoulder should be closest to the net and your left arm extended and pointing up at the shuttle. Your weight will shift to the right leg as you prepare for the shot and take your backswing, then shift to the left foot as the stroke is taken.

Bring the racket up to meet the shuttle as high as possible. The shuttle is contacted above and in front of your shoulder, not out to the side. It is hit at the highest point possible. At contact, your arm straightens, and your wrist snaps quickly. The racket head will be facing upward slightly at contact. Let the racket continue outward and to the left side of your body. When you shift your weight to your forward foot, keep your forward knee slightly flexed for balance.

The overhead clear shot should drop perpendicular to the floor and land between the baseline and the long doubles service line. This deep shot, which drops straight down, is more difficult for your opponent to hit. If you have time, look at your opponent's feet to see if they are near the baseline, which is a good indication that your clear is deep.

You will note that the shuttle does not follow the same path as a ball would follow. A ball will follow an arc path—with the angle of ascent and descent approximately the same. The shuttle, because it is so light and has great air resistance almost immediately slows down, then drop nearly straight down. Because of its unusual flight path, beginners often have trouble anticipating where the shuttle will drop.

A good clear will also give you more time to get back to home base (in the center of your court) and will make it more difficult for your opponent to smash effectively, because one cannot smash effectively from deep in one's court. Remember to return to your home base and be in your ready position after each shot.

When you can hit the clear consistently you may want to play a *long and short game.* In this game you will try to keep your opponent back most of the time while occasionally hitting a drop shot to break his or her playing rhythm.

> **Checklist for the High Clear Shot**
>
> 1. Are you in the ready position?
>
> 2. Do you have a forehand grip?
>
> 3. Are you behind the shuttle with your left shoulder pointing to it?
>
> 4. Is your racket pointed downward behind your back with your wrist cocked?
>
> 5. As you swing upward do you contact the shuttle in front of your body with a hard wrist snap, hitting the shuttle high?
>
> 6. Do you follow through completely?

Throwing Drill for Beginners

To learn the arm action for overhead strokes, follow this drill. Start without your racket. Your intention is to throw the shuttle up and out as far as possible. This throwing action is very similar to that used in hitting the clear or the smash.

Turn your body, and face the sidelines with your left shoulder toward the net. With your left foot forward (for right-handers) and weight on your back foot, take the shuttle in your right hand and hold it at the base. Bring your right elbow to shoulder height and away from your body. Your hand and the shuttle should be behind your right ear. Your wrist should be flexed toward the thumb side of your hand. Now throw the shuttle *up and out* as far as you can reach.

Transfer your weight to your forward (left) foot as you release the shuttle. Your upper torso will rotate to your left as your arm comes upward and forward. Try throwing a few more times to get the overall sensation. Check your release

Throwing drill

Try throwing a few more times to get the overall sensation. Check your release in relation to your body with your best throws. This is the angle at which you want your racket to contact the shuttle.

Practice hint Occasionally while rallying have the opposite player let the shuttle drop so that you can see if it lands near the baseline. This is where a good defensive clear should fall.

Hint for advanced players: In order to get back to the center of the court quickly, advanced players should "scissor" their legs as they hit the high clear shot. In this technique the weight is shifted from the racket-side leg to the other leg as the shuttle is hit. The player gets under the shuttle, jumps upward from the racket-side leg, and then, after hitting the shuttle, lands on the other leg and moves forward toward the home-base position.

Backhand Overhead Clear

The *backhand overhead clear* is used mainly in singles when the player cannot get in position to hit a forehand. Always make the forehand shot if possible. For the backhand clear you must turn your body completely to the backhand side so that you are facing your left sideline. Your right shoulder should be toward the net and your right foot pointed diagonally toward the left net post. Your elbow should be pointing at the oncoming shuttle. The shuttle should be away from the body so that a circular swing can be made. (This is different from the forehand clear, which is hit directly over the shoulder.) This shot will require more backswing from the shoulder because the muscles in the back of the forearm (which supply the power for backhand shots) are not as strong as those in the front of the forearm, which supply the power to forehand shots.

The shuttle is contacted high and in front of your body. Your weight will shift to your right foot as you hit and follow through.

Backhand clear:

**A. Backswing   B. Foreswing   C. Contact   D. Follow-
hrough**

Attacking clear:

A. Backswing

C.   D. F

Attacking Clear

The *attacking clear* is used when your opponent is close to the net, and you think you can get the shuttle over his or her head for a winner. It is hit like a clear except that the trajectory is lower.

Smash

The *smash* is the most powerful stroke in badminton. It is hit extremely hard and, if hit effectively, usually ends the rally. However, speed is not always as important as the downward angle. Body position is the same as for the clear, the difference being in the angle of the racket at the contact point. In the clear the racket head is pointed up, while in the smash it is angled down. A second difference is the increased speed of your forearm and wrist snap.

As you get set for the smash, your left shoulder should be closest to the net. The shuttle should be ahead of your hitting shoulder—much farther ahead than where you contact the clear. (The weaker your wrist, the further forward the shuttle should be hit.) You should hit the shuttle in front of your shoulder and at the highest point possible. Your shoulder, forearm, and wrist will rotate rapidly forward as the shuttle is contacted. Hitting it slightly ahead of your body will give your shot a sharper angle.

Footwork for scissors kick in smash

Backhand smash:

A. Backswing   B. **Foreswing**

61

C. Contact   D. Follow-through

As you hit the smash, your upper body should move forward and downward. This facilitates power and follow-through. If you are behind the middle of the court, your forward momentum helps you to get back into the home-base position more quickly and get set for a possible return.

The smash should land near either sideline and at approximately mid-court-10 to 16 feet from the net.

Use this shot only when you expect it to be a winner. Since you are expending a great deal of energy, and you may be off-balance after your follow-through, it is important that it be done effectively.

The smash should be used only when you are in the front three-quarters of the court unless you are a very strong player. Beyond that area your opponent will probably have time to return it, because the shuttle will lose speed as it flies the greater distance, and your opponent can see the shuttle for a longer period of time. But if you have a chance to hit a smash when you are in the forecourt area, there is a very good chance that it will be a winner.

If you find that you are smashing into the net, it means that either you are hitting the shuttle too far in front of you or that you have an exceptionally strong wrist snap. In either case, move under the shuttle a bit more, so that it is not so far in front of you before you hit it. If you are hitting out of bounds, you will need to hit the shuttle farther in front of your body or use more wrist snap.

The smash is probably the most overused stroke in the game—especially among the younger players. The best strategy is almost always to move your opponent up and back, side to side, and wait patiently for the opening for a smash that will be a winner and end the rally.

You can occasionally hit a smash at your opponent's body. The chest-to-hip area on the racket-side of your opponent is most vulnerable to this type of shot.

Checklist for the Smash
1. Are you facing the right sideline?
2. Is your racket pointed down behind your back in the backswing?
3. Do you swing high, then contact the shuttle in front of your body with a hard, downward wrist snap?
4. Do you shift your weight to your left foot as you complete a full follow-through?

Half-Smash

The half-smash is an attacking stroke used in singles, doubles, and mixed doubles. It is hit similarly to the smash, but placement rather than speed is the essential. The power will come more from the wrist snap than from the whole body.

This shot provides a good change of pace. It is essential to place it to the side of the court and with a sharp downward trajectory so that your opponent cannot reach it.

The halfcourt smash, which lands about midcourt, is often more effective than the full smash, which may land deep in your opponent's backcourt. Actually, both shots should be used. When you play both, you keep your opponent guessing as to whether to move up or back to cover your shot.

Drop Shot

The *drop shot* is a soft shot that barely clears the net, then lands close to the net on the other side—preferably in one of the front corners. It is used to move your opponent forward and to force an upward return that may give you the opportunity for a smash shot. It can be used effectively when your opponent is deep or expects a smash.

The arm action for the drop shot should look like the clear—and vice versa—so that you can disguise your shots and thus surprise your opponent. Use the combination of clear and drop to move your opponent back and forward. This will cause fatigue and will often keep him or her off-balance. Remember that deception is the key. In the drop shot, the shuttle is contacted in front of the body and the speed of the racket at the time of the hit is greatly slowed compared to the clear. The racket head should be perpendicular to the floor or slightly past the perpendicular.

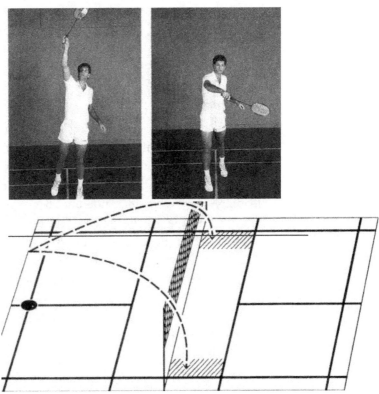

The swing speed should start fast to look like a clear or a smash, but the elbow and wrist snap should be slow as you softly guide the shuttle over the net with your follow-through. If you fail to disguise this shot, your opponent will be able to get the jump on you and make an easy play. Many beginners look like the Statue of Liberty—standing motionless during this shot, a dead giveaway.

Rather than arcing up and coming down, the trajectory of the shuttle should start immediately down from the racket and fall into your opponent's forecourt just past the net. The lower you have to reach to contact the shuttle, and the farther you have to hit it, the more you will have to open the face of the racket upward.

Drop shots can be hit very soft and land just past the net or they can be hit harder, dropping a bit farther from the net. The softness of the shot will be determined by how much of the wrist snap you eliminate as you are contacting the shuttle and making your follow-through.

Push or Dab Shot

The *push,* or *dab,* is used at the net, primarily in doubles play. It is more of a sidearm block than an overhead shot, hit downward with little or no backswing. The elbow is flexed and held in front of the body. You lunge at the shuttle with your racket-side leg leading. The wrist does not uncock as you push the shuttle, and the follow-through will be very short. You are looking for placement rather than speed in this shot, the most effective placement being near midcourt, between the opponents, and to the sideline.

Timing is very important on the push stroke, which is used primarily in doubles. It is most effective against a team playing up and back.

Dab:

Forehand Drive

For the forehand drive, use your forehand grip and swing in a circular path, whipping your wrist as you contact the shuttle. The contact point is diagonally in front of your left foot. Play it at as high a point as possible so that you will not be hitting up at the shuttle.

Be sure that you are not crowding the shuttle by getting too close. You want to be able to swing freely at it. Your follow-through will be around your body. Your arm and racket will have completed about three-fourths of a circle.

For the backhand drive shot, you use a backhand grip and less wrist but more elbow movement. As you get set for the shot, turn your body so that you are facing the left sideline. Make your backswing with much more elbow bend than in the regular drive shot. Then, with your right elbow pointing at the oncoming shuttle, shift your weight to your right foot as you swing with your shoulders, arm, and wrist. Hit the shuttle in front of you, then follow through around your body.

Your drives can be played down the near sideline or crosscourt—depending on where your opponent has left an opening. Your shots should be hit hard, in a path parallel to the floor—just clearing the net. If your opponent is forced to play your drive while it is still moving fast, there is less likelihood of an effective return. And if it is not played quickly and begins to drop, your opponent will be forced to hit up, giving you the advantage here, too.

Round-the-Head Shot

More advanced players often hit what is called a *round-the-head* shot. Clears, smashes, and drops can all be hit with this stroking action, which is done to avoid having to take a shot on the backhand side (a weaker or a defensive shot). A round-the-head shot allows you to stay on the attack.

Your grip will be a forehand grip—although some players prefer a frying-pan grip. The shot will be made with your body facing the net or while you are jumping to get better height. The backswing is similar to other overhead shots, but the contact point is above your left shoulder.

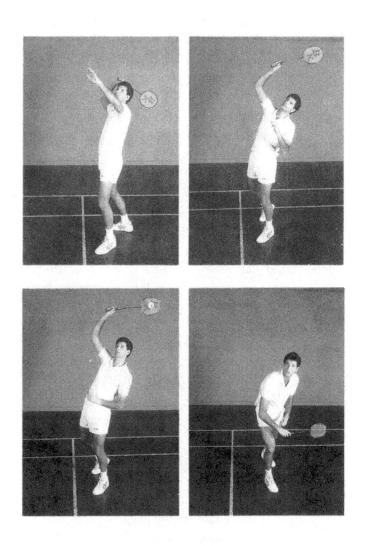

If your feet are on the floor, your weight should be on the left foot. If you jump for the shot, you should scissor your legs (a *switch step)*, getting your right leg forward, to allow you to get back to your home-base position more quickly.

Summary

1. For all overhead strokes, the direction of the shuttle will be determined by the angle of the racket at the time of contact. So when practicing, concentrate on which racket angle gives you the exact trajectory that you want.

2. Get behind the shuttle as quickly as you can to better enable you to make the kind of shot that you want to make.

3. Always try to take the offense when your opponent hits you a high shot—especially one that is high and short.

4. Always contact the shuttle as high as possible.

5. The major overhead shots are
- Forehand overhead clear.
- Backhand overhead clear.
- Drop shot.
- Smash.
- Half-smash.
- Dab or push.
- Forehand drive.
- Backhand drive.
- Round-the-head shots.

CHAPTER 7

Underhand Strokes and Smash Returns

Outline
Forehand Underhand Clear
Defensing the Smash
Backhand Underhand Clear
Hairpin Drop or Dribble
Checklist for the Underhand Clear
Checklist for the Hairpin Drop
Underhand Drop
Summary

While you would prefer to hit all of your shots downward, using overhead strokes, your opponents will often catch you with a drop shot or smash, and then you will have to hit underhanded. In doing so, you will be playing a defensive game. You will therefore want to keep your opponent off-balance by hitting the shuttle deep in a clearing shot or having the shuttle drop close to the net.

The underhand shots are
- Underhand clear.
- Underhand drop.
- Hairpin drop.

As in all badminton shots, you want to hit the shuttle at the highest point possible.

Forehand Underhand Clear

When your opponent makes an effective drop shot into your forecourt, you must go on the defensive—so it is best to hit an underhand clear. This will force your opponent into the backcourt and give you time to get back to your home-base position.

Assuming that the shuttle is dropping toward your forehand side, get to the shuttle as fast as you can. Your first step will be a short one with the left leg. Your right leg should then come forward with a long enough step to bring you to the shuttle.

Reach for the shuttle. Getting too close will inhibit your swing. Bring your racket down and under the oncoming shuttle. Your wrist should be slightly cocked.

Contact the shuttle in front of your body with your weight on your forward foot. Swing the racket upward while uncocking your wrist and whipping it through the shuttle. Follow through in the direction that you intend the shuttle to go. It should land within 2 feet of your opponent's baseline, and its flight should resemble that of a high singles serve.

Remember to step with your right foot. This will extend your reach by about 1 foot. It will also allow you to get back to your home base more quickly to get ready for the next shot.

https://vimeo.com/288044741/93b0ea7b32On crosscourt shots, contact the shuttle harder in order to make up the extra distance it will have to travel.

Backhand Underhand Clear

On strokes made from your non-racket side, change to a backhand grip. Your last step as you reach for the shuttle will be with your right foot. Get to the shuttle as soon as possible. Your racket should be in line with and behind

Backhand underhand clear:

the shuttle. As you contact it, your forearm and wrist should whip your racket through the shuttle as you follow through in the intended direction of the flight of the shuttle. It should travel high and to the baseline area.

Underhand Drop

The underhand drop is played from behind the front service line. It is very similar to a low serve in that it should just clear the net, then drop quickly. This shot is valuable primarily in doubles play when played from midcourt. It can force a net player to move from side to side, or it can bring backcourt players to the net if they are playing side by side. In singles, it is generally used to return a smash, forcing the smashing player to cover some distance, then go on the defensive by hitting up.

Defensing the Smash

Defensing the smash is started by dropping your racket head low when you see that a smash is coming. It is best accomplished by *blocking* the smash crosscourt. (Your return may be a sidearm or an underhand stroke.)

The *block shot* is like the dab shot. It should land close to the net. Since it requires no backswing, you can use it to make the return even if you just barely get to the smash. If you don't have time to aim it, just block it straight. Your short shot will still give your opponent trouble.

A backhand shot gives you a greater range of blocking area—from shots aimed at the midline of your body to the non-racket sideline. With a forehand you have a range from in front of your racket-side leg to the sideline on your racket side.

Your return of the smash should get the shuttle back to an area that is difficult for your opponent to cover. Keep your opponent off-balance with a mix of drops, clears, and drives.

Also, smashes must be returned quickly; or the speed of the shuttle will have it past you in an instant.

The quickness required for your smash returns will limit you to primarily wrist shots. You won't have time to wind up and take a full backswing. Keep your opponent guessing as to where you will return your shot. In singles you will generally use a blocking action to return a smash, the *hairpin drop,* or *dribble,* is made close to the net after your opponent has hit a drop shot to you. The idea is to lift the shuttle gently over the top of the net and have it drop as close to the net as possible.

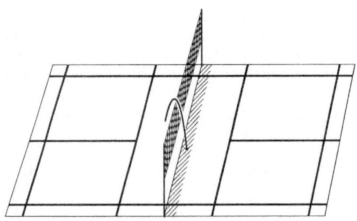

Get to the shuttle quickly, so that you can contact the shuttle as close to the top of the net as possible. In singles you don't have to be quite as precise with your placement as you do in doubles.

Your grip should be loose. Step toward the shuttle with your racket-side foot. The stroke is executed with your forearm and wrist. You should guide the shuttle over the net gently, and follow through with your forearm to give the desired direction.

You can place the shuttle directly in front of where you contact it, or you can guide it to a front corner of the court. Its flight path will be determined by the angle of your racket head at the point of contact.

Keep the shuttle close to the top of the net so that it cannot be smashed back at you. It should just clear the net and then drop. It is very difficult to return.

In doubles, with one person playing up and one back, you will be closer to the shuttle on this type of shot—but so is your opponent. You will have more area next to the net toward which to aim. You will need more variation and deception in your technique in order to hit safely to any spot in the forecourt. For that reason, when playing doubles you may want to *choke* up on your grip a bit (slide your hand up the handle) for better control.

Checklist for Hairpin Drop
1. Hold the racket loosely with a forehand grip.
2. Step with the right foot toward the shuttle.
3. Gently guide the shuttle over the net—as close to the top of the net as possible.

Summary
1. While it is always preferable to hit with an overhead stroke, a good opponent will force you to hit many shots underhand.

2. Always try to use your underhand shot to get your opponent off-balance and to force a return to you that is high and short.

3. An effective drop shot at the net forces your opponent to hit the shuttle up. This may give you a set-up for a smash or a drive.

4. A high clear to your opponent can put him or her on the defensive.

5. One of the most effective shots to counter your opponent's drop shot is the dribble or hairpin drop.

6. On smash returns, block the shuttle as far in front of you as possible.

In providing videos of actual games, you can get an idea of both how the various shots are made in competitiom and the strategies that players use to put their opponents off balance. Deep to short, right to left, forehand to backhand. This video records the longest rally in men's single championship competition—more than 70 shots! Click:.

https://vimeo.com/288044873/69f24945a7

CHAPTER 8

Strategy

Outline
Basic Strategy
Your Fundamental Shots
Developing Game Strategy During Warm-Up
Singles Strategy
Singles Serving
Return of Service for Singles
Singles Rally Strategy
Checklist for Singles Strategy
Doubles Strategy
Doubles Serving
Defensive Strategy for Doubles Offensive Strategy for Doubles Combination Strategy
Checklist for Doubles Strategy
Mixed Doubles Strategy *Mixed Doubles Serving Return of Service for Mixed Doubles Mixed Doubles Play*
Checklist for Mixed Doubles Strategy
Summary

One of the major thrills of badminton is outsmarting your opponent. Wise strategic decisions, if properly executed with good fundamentals, will win many games. As you gain experience and expertise, you will have more strategic options. In this chapter we will look at strategy from the beginning level to the more advanced levels.

Basic Strategy

1. Keep the shuttle away from your opponent.
2. Move your opponent out of the center of the court (the home-base position).
3. When in doubt, place the shuttle behind your opponent and hope for a weak return.
4. The backhand is usually the weaker side, so play to that.
5. While it is obvious that a left-hander's backhand is the same side as a right-hander's forehand, people often forget this. Remember to avoid hitting toward the forehand of a left-handed opponent under the mistaken notion that it is his or her backhand.
6. Return to your home-base position after every shot.
7. Use the smash to finish rallies, not as a basic shot to move your opponent and create openings.

Your Fundamental Shots

Good strategic decisions are wasted without good fundamentals. Remember these key points:
- Try always to hit the shuttle at as high a point as possible and as soon as possible. Don't wait

for the shuttle to come to you. Move to it quickly and get behind it.

• Deception is a key element in this game, so you should attempt to make your strokes look similar as long as possible. For example, when a shot is hit high, you can fake a drop and hit a clear, or fake a smash and hit a drop.

Developing Game Strategy During Warm-Up

Try out various shots on your opponent during warm-up to see how he or she reacts to them. Especially try (1) drops to check your opponent's speed and ability and (2) clears to the backhand side to check on his or her strength there—and also to see if he or she runs around the backhand, thereby opening up an area to the forehand side.

Note whether your opponent seems slow or lazy. Is there a pattern to his or her returns, such as always hitting straight or crosscourt, or always clearing or dropping? Does your opponent want to smash too often, even when out of position or off-balance? These observations will help you plan your strategy.

If you are in a tournament, watch your future opponents in their matches to discover their strengths and weaknesses.

Target areas for singles: 1, 3 clears; 1, 4 drives; 2 drops

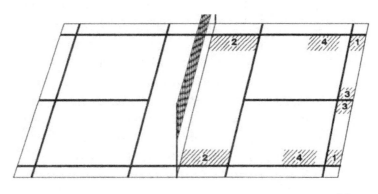

Singles Strategy

Most of your singles serves will be high and deep (whereas most of your doubles serves will be low and short). Throw in some flicks and drives, but mix them up so that your opponent cannot anticipate them. Try to be deceptive on your serves as well as on your strokes. And remember that if your serves are fast, the returns from your opponent are likely to be fast, so be ready for them.

Singles Serving

Singles serving is usually a high, deep shot to the back of the court near the midline. By serving near the midline of the backcourt, you cut down on the angle that your opponent can hit. But, again, vary your serves so that your opponent cannot guess exactly what you will do.

If your opponent is playing a bit too deep, hit a short serve. And if he or she is playing too close, hit the high, clear serve. Watch for evidence that one particular serve gives your opponent trouble.

Return of Service for Singles

Generally at the beginning level you will return both serves and shots straight ahead rather than placing them crosscourt, since the crosscourt shot takes longer and gives your opponent more time to adjust. Also, being a longer shot, it is more likely to fall shorter than intended and give your opponent an opening for a smash. But don't be predictable. You want to keep your opponent off-balance and guessing.

Your service return should move your opponent away from center court. The only time you would use a smash on a service return is on a high, short serve. Even then, use the smash only if you are certain that you can "put the bird on the floor." If you try to smash an effective serve, you will probably hit it weak, and you will be the one at a disadvantage.

The returns you'll use most often for a high serve are a high clear or a drop in the near corner away from your opponent. If a high serve is short (in front of the back doubles service line) you may smash, hit an attacking clear, or a drop to either near corner. If your opponent serves short and low, your best returns are a drop to the near corner or a flick or attacking clear, provided your opponent is close to the front service line.

Singles Rally Strategy

A primary rule of rally strategy is that whenever you get in trouble, you should hit the clear to your opponent's backhand. This gives you time to recover and may force your opponent into a weak return.

If you can get your opponent moving forward and back you will have an advantage. Try to move him or her into the various corners of the court and away from the controlling position in the center of the court. By moving your opponent, you may force weak returns and create holes in his or her defense. For you to keep control of the rally, you must maintain your strong position at your home base.

A popular combination is a clear to the backhand, then a drop to the forehand, followed by another deep backhand clear and another forehand drop. This makes your opponent move a great distance and execute a weak shot (the high backhand) at the end of a long run.

With a continued pattern of clears and drops, you will eventually force your opponent to hit a weak return. This is the time for you to win the point with a smash. You must have both patience and endurance for this defensive type of strategy. Once you get your opponent moving, you can take the offensive. Vary your shots. You can hit a hard drive or a smash directly at your opponent as he or she charges the net. If your

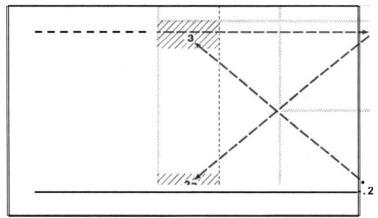

opponent runs quickly forward after you have hit a clear, you might hit two clears in a row. You can then hit a drive behind your opponent as he or she is moving in the opposite direction.

While every player should be adept at both offensive shots and defensive shots, before starting serious training you should determine whether you want to emphasize the offensive or defensive aspects of your game. Which style fits you best?

If you are strong and can hit hard, you may opt to be an attacking player. If you are quick, have stamina, and perhaps are shorter than average, you might choose to play a more defensive game. In either case you will need to practice all of your fundamentals, because the offensive players will use many clears and drops, and the defensive players will sometimes use the smash.

To defend a smash, block it, and drop it close to the net. If your opponent has smashed straight, you might drop it crosscourt. If your opponent has smashed crosscourt, drop it in the near front corner.

If you are trailing your opponent's score late in a game, you might switch your strategy to a safer one called the *center court them'*, in which you avoid the sidelines in your shots. Hit smashes at your opponent's body—between the waist and shoulder of the racket side of the body. Such a strategy reduces your chance of hitting the shuttle out of bounds, and it reduces the angle of return by your opponent. (Note: This is an exception to the badminton courtesy of avoiding hits into the body of an opponent as a common practice.)

Doubles Strategy

Doubles is a more complex game than singles. It demands faster reactions and being able to anticipate what your partner and your opponents will do with the shuttle. Good doubles play begins with an effective serve or service return (the most important parts of the game) and ends with good teamwork on offense.

Doubles Serving

The server in a doubles game must vary the placement of the serve in order to prevent the opponent from attacking the serve. The short serve, the drive, and the high flick serves are used in doubles. The low, short serve to the near corner (the diagonal "7 area) is the most common serve. Top-caliber servers can often make points with a shot that is generally thought to be defensive.

Deception, an essential in the game of badminton, is particularly important in the serve. Make certain that the beginning of your serving action is the same for every type of serve you execute.

Return of Service for Doubles

The return for beginners should start with the ready position taken a few feet back from the front service line. As you become advanced, you will move up to within one foot of the front service line and within one foot of the centerline. From this point any low serves can be played quickly and at a high point.

Drop returns should be played straight ahead, not crosscourt. Drive returns should be at the backhand or down the near sideline. Push returns should be at the near sideline and to midcourt.

Target areas for doubles:
1. Low serves
2. Flicks and drive serves
3. Drop shots
4. Drives and smashes
5. Half smashes and pushes

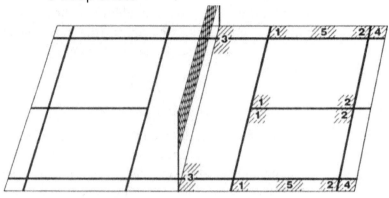

The best service returns for doubles are
- A push along the near sideline to midcourt.
- A drop shot away from the server's side.
- A drive to the deep corner on the near side.
- A push shot just behind the server.
- A push into the body of the server's partner.

Defensive Strategy for Doubles

Effective service, service return, and rallies in doubles play all begin with proper alignment. Start your play from the best position for what you want to accomplish. You can play a defensive alignment *(side by side)*, an offensive alignment *(up and back)*, or you can use a combination of these two formations, called *circular rotation,* depending on the situation in the game.

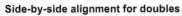

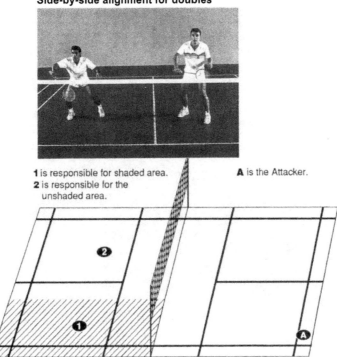

1 is responsible for shaded area.
2 is responsible for the unshaded area.

A is the Attacker.

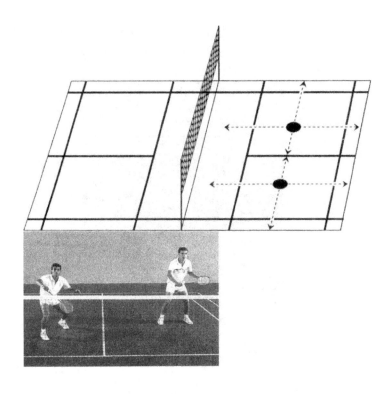

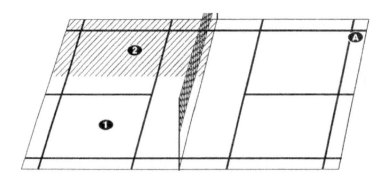

Side by side   (A is attacker)
2 is responsible for shaded area, 1 for unshaded area.

In the *side-by-side alignment,* the basic defensive position for doubles, each partner is responsible for his or her half of the court. This

88

alignment is easy to learn and eliminates confusion as to who will take a shot.

The defender directly in front of the attacker takes all shuttles that are hit to the sideline, all drop shots to his or her side of the court, all shots at the body, and all the high clears down the middle. The partner, who turns slightly toward the attacker, takes all the smashes hit to the center of the court or crosscourt and all drop shots on his or her side of the court.

This side-by-side alignment makes it much more difficult for your opponents to smash effectively. A drawback, however, is that it allows your opponents to continue to play to the weaker partner, not only obtaining weaker returns but also tiring him or her. Also, as a defensive rather than an offensive formation, it reduces a team's chance to attack, and doubles is an offensive game.

To get back on offense, a team using this alignment should block or push its opponents' smashes into the half court area or clear them crosscourt. The attacker should be forced to run sideways to maintain his or her attack. This way he or she will not be able to hit deep, angled smashes, and hence the defenders will have a better chance of playing halfcourt returns and getting back on offense.

Side-by-side alignment is the best strategy when your opponents are in control. However, it should be remembered that attacking (offensive strategy) rather than defending is generally the best plan for winning at doubles.

Offensive Strategy for Doubles

The *up-and-back alignment* for offensive play places both players in the midline of the court with one player close to the net, about one foot behind the "T" (the intersection of the midline and the short service line) and the other playing deep. This alignment (also easy to learn) is more effective against a team that hits strong, deep clears and short drops. One of its advantages is that the weaker player can be "hidden" at the net, with the stronger player playing most of the court. Another is that it is an attacking that the sides of the court are open to the smash and your opponents can run the backcourt player from side to side to tire him or her.

The normal pattern is for the server to play the "up" position after serving. The person receiving will play up if the serve is short and will play deep if the serve is long—with the partner playing the opposite position. In more advanced doubles the stronger person will generally play deep and the weaker person up.

Up-Back Formation disadvantages are;

Both players must keep the shuttle low to the opponents. Any time that the shuttle is hit high the net player becomes a sitting duck for a smash.

When playing the up-and-back alignment, if you are the up player do not turn and look toward your partner. Keep your eyes on your opponents. There are two reasons for this. One is that you can get hit in the face with your partner's shot. The other is that by watching your opponents, you will know where the shuttle is going and will be able to adjust to its return more quickly.

The deeper player should adjust his or her position by playing slightly to the other side of the court from the up person. So if the up player is forced to the right, the back player will move to the left.

The success of offensive doubles depends to a large degree on the person playing near the net. This player can block shots and drop them close to the net—forcing the opponents into weak returns. Most rallies in good doubles are won by the net player.

The net player should take a position one and one-half to two feet ahead of the short service line. The racket should be held near net level. From this position you can move side to side and cut off most short shots. On a smash the forecourt player should defend the opposite side of the court from where the attacker is. This means that the forecourt player moves away from the centerline and back behind the short service line (see diagram).

From this position the forecourt player should be able to make downward shots that the attackers will have to pop up. If it is not possible to hit the shuttle down, it should be blocked near the net to keep the opponents on the defensive.

The backcourt player should attempt to hit smashes down the line, into the center of the court, or into the body of the opponent who is nearest. The speed and angle of the smash should be varied to keep the opponents off-balance. Power is not as important in winning at doubles as variety and consistency.

Partners should be able to adjust to each other and to the expected shots of their opponents. For example, if the net player has hit a drop shot, the backcourt player can move up, expecting that the opponents will counter with another drop shot.

Experienced players will be able to see if their opponents have moved forward or are too far back. They can then adjust their shots to take advantage of the resulting openings. Players who have played together for a long time will learn their partners' strengths and weaknesses and be able to set up their partners so that they make strong shots.

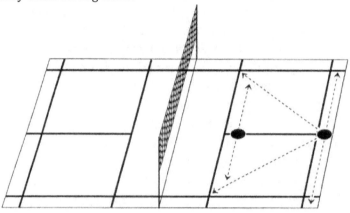

Combination Strategy

Combination of the side-by-side and up-and-back strategies is possible for more advanced players. As you get to know your partner, you can switch between side-by-side and up-and back- formations. Usually, if you hit the shuttle down, as in a drop, smash, or drive, you will go on offense and play up and back. If you lift the shuttle, you will likely go on defense and play side-by-side. A lower-level player may use verbal signals to alert the partner to a change, but advanced players learn to react to the proper position depending on the shot.

1. Against an up-and-back team

Play to the weaker opponent. Hit shots to the corners to make opponents move sideways and to hit weaker returns or hit up.

    a. Smash to the sidelines as often as possible.

    b. Hit shots to the corners to make opponents move up and back.

2. Against a side-by-side team

    a. Hit midcourt level shots to the sidelines.

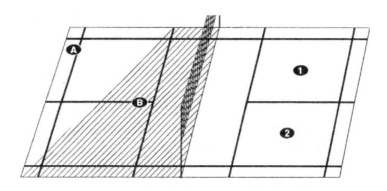

A is responsible for unshaded area.
B is responsible for the shaded area.

Mixed Doubles Strategy

At the championship level men are generally stronger, taller, and faster than women. In physical education classes these differences may not exist. For this reason mixed doubles strategy will be discussed in terms of the stronger and weaker player rather than the man and the woman.

Mixed Doubles Serving

The basic serve in mixed doubles is the short serve. However, doubles players should also have an effective flick serve in order to be able to take advantage of any weaknesses in the opponents' alignment or fundamental skills.

The short serve is usually served to the "T" (the intersection of the front service line with the midline.) A wide short serve to the side of the court is usually not employed because the *down-the-line* return of serve is simple to execute and difficult to defend against.

A flick serve can be used more often against the shorter and weaker (and therefore probably slower) player, from the usual position at the net. It may also create gaps in the defense and allow the serving team to "put the bird on the floor."

The weaker player, who will be covering the shots close to the net, will serve from close to the front service line. The stronger player may serve from deeper in order to be ready for a high, clear return.

Return of Service for Mixed Doubles

The return of service is very important in mixed doubles. If the serve is poor (i.e., too high at the net) the receiver should move quickly to hit the shuttle down. The best return is usually straight back into the server at waist level and into the racket side of the body.

If the stronger player serves short and tight to the weaker opponent, the returner can make a net return to the sideline. A crosscourt net return might be intercepted by the opposing net player. Other times the shuttle can be pushed into the deep corners of the court before the stronger player is able to get back to cover them.

If the weaker player is serving to the weaker player on the other team, the returns should be straight ahead or dropped into the corner away from the server. Any crosscourt returns can be intercepted by the server and dabbed to the floor.

Short returns to the outside corners should be returned straight, regardless of who is serving.

In high-level competition, when the stronger player returns a serve from the weaker opponent, the shuttle should be pushed into the face or body of the weaker opponent. Another effective return is the halfcourt push to the sidelines. Avoid making a net shot straight ahead, because it can be cleared quickly over the stronger player's head, forcing the weaker partner to go into the backcourt.

When the stronger player returns service from an opposing strong player, the shuttle should be pushed to the sidelines at about halfcourt depth. It is most important for the stronger player to hit the return downward. After the return, the stronger player should move quickly to the backcourt to protect that area. The strongest alignment in mixed doubles is to have the weaker player up and the stronger player back. This puts the team in the best offensive position.

When either partner receives a flick serve, it should be smashed to the sidelines or into the server's body. Once in a while a fast drop or half-smash at the alley can be attempted.

Mixed Doubles Play

The play in mixed doubles should be concentrated toward the sidelines because the partners will be generally playing up and back. The shuttle should be hit down to make the opponents hit upward. If you are forced to hit a high, clear shot, move into *a wedge formation*, because your opponents will probably hit a smash. In the wedge formation the stronger player aligns in front of the smasher and fairly deep in the court. The responsibility is for all shots to that side of the court. The weaker player defends the other side of the court and aligns shorter to take crosscourt and midcourt shots and drops. The racket should be held in front of the body with the head of the racket at head height.

Try to move the net player, usually the weaker player, from side to side with fast drops and crosscourt net shots. The shuttle should be played flat and directed down the sidelines. Crosscourt flat shots can be easily cut off by the opposing net player. However, if the deep player wants to hit a crosscourt shot, it should be hit over the head of the opposing net player to push him or her into the backcourt.

The net player, in general, should not try to intercept the straight halfcourt pushes unless he or she is certain of a good return. The net player should be content playing a good net game by hitting low net shots—not by hitting clears. When the shuttle is returned a bit higher than the top of the net, it should be smashed. The net player should hit every shot down, whether it be a drop, a drive, or a push.

On defense a wedge formation can be used when you have hit a high, weak return and expect a smash. The weaker player moves back a few steps and takes a position to intercept crosscourt smashes and drops. The smashes should be blocked away from the opposing net player.

1. Play to the near sidelines.

2. Move the net player from side to side.

3. Try to hit every shot down.

4. Most serves should be low.

Summary

1. Simple strategy includes
 a. Keeping the shuttle away from your opponent.
 b. Moving your opponent from the home-base position.
 c. When in doubt, hitting a high clear to your opponent's backhand.
2. Singles serving strategy is based on serving mostly high deep serves.
3. Singles strategy is designed to keep your opponent away
4. The smash is the most overused stroke in badminton.
5. Doubles is a more complex game than singles.
6. The serve is the most important part of a doubles game. Serves should be short and low or higher flick serves. Keep your opponent off-balance.
7. The side-by-side alignment is a defensive formation.
8. The up-and-back alignment is an offensive formation.

When you think you are ready—here are some crazy badminton shot! Click:

https://vimeo.com/288044741/93b0ea7b32

CHAPTER 9
Drills

Outline

Drills
1. Serving Drills
2. High Service Return Drills
3. Low Service Return Drills
4. Straight Clear
5. Crosscourt Clear
6. Combination Down-the-Line and Crosscourt Drills
7. Overhead Clear-and-Drop Combination
8. Smash Drill
9. Smash-and-Block Drill
10. Smash-and-Halfcourt Drive
11. Drives
12. Drops Alternating Drops
13. Overhead Drop and Underhand Clear
14. Net Shots (Hairpin Drops and Cross-Net Shots)
15. Quickness Drill
1Z Clear, Smash, Drop, Clear
18. Doubles Drill Self-Tests
 1. Deep Singles Serves
 2. Low Doubles Serve
 3. Forehand and Backhand Clears
 4. Drop Shots
 5. Smash Summary

Drills

In any sport the best players are the ones who work the most on their fundamental skills. Badminton is no exception. The more you practice, the more you will improve your game. Here are some drills to incorporate into your practice sessions.

1. Serving Drills

This drill can be done with or without a partner. The server simply hits the desired serve, high clear, short, flick, or drive), and the partner—if there is one—lets the shuttle drop to see how close to the desired corner it lands. When doing this drill alone, use several shuttles.

2. High Service Return Drills

A partner is required to serve a high clear. It is returned with the smash, clear, or drop.

3. Low Service Return Drills

A partner is required to serve a low serve to either front corner of the doubles court. Taking the proper alignment near the front service line, and close to the centerline, you return the serve with the underhand clear, drive, push, drop, or rushing-net shot.

4. Straight Clear

Partners hit to each other, from the backcourt then from the forecourt, attempting to get the shuttle to drop straight down within one foot of the bacldine. Every so often, a player can let the shuttle drop to see just how close it was to the baseline.

5. Crosscourt Clear

Players both hit crosscourt clears, working for distance and placement into the corner box—the area between the singles and doubles sidelines and the deep doubles service line and the basely ne. This drill should be done forehand to forehand or, for advanced players, backhand to backhand.

6. Combination Down-the-Line and Crosscourt Clears

1. Players start in home-base position and hit down-the-line clears, returning to home base after each shot.

2. Players start in home-base position and hit crosscourt clears, returning to home base after each shot.

3. Players alternate between down-the-line and crosscourt shots, returning to home base after each shot.

7. Overhead Clear-and-Drop Combination

One player hits all clears while the other alternates between hitting an overhead clear and a drop. Emphasis with the advanced players should be to disguise the shots so that the windup of the backswing and the forward swing look similar.

Smash **drill (8)**

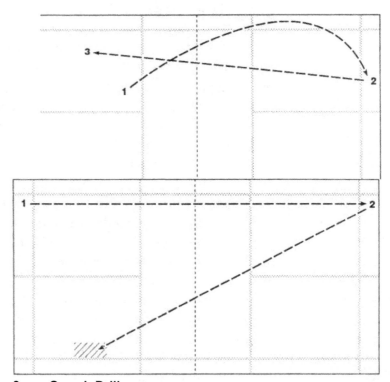

8. Smash Drill

One player hits short, high clears while the other smashes.

9. Smash-and-Block Drill

One player hits a short, high clears, which the partner smashes. The returner attempts to block the smash straight ahead.

10. Smash-and-Halfcourt Drive

Similar to the smash-and block drill, but the returner applies more power to the return and hits a halfcourt drive.

11. Drives

Each player hits drive drives to each other down the near sideline. One player's forehand shot will be played by the other's backhand.

Partners hit drops, straight and crosscourt, to each other straight ahead. They then work on the crosscourt drop. The shuttle should just clear the net on each shot.

12. Alternating Drops

Both persons hit drops alternately.

13. Overhead Drop and Underhand Clear

One player hits only drops, while the partner hits only clears.

14. Net Shots (Hairpin Drops and Cross-Net Shots) Players practice hairpin drops, then crosscourt net shots, then hit them in combination—trying to score on the other net player.

15. Quickness Drill

Players stand on the "r and hit drive shots at and to each other. One can hit all forehands while the other hits all backhands. They can then rally as quickly as possible, hitting all drives (no clears or drops). By hitting some drives at each other, they can learn how to defend against this type of shot. This drill helps the player learn how to watch the shuttle and react quickly.

17. Clear, Smash, Drop, Clear

One player hits a clear, the partner returns it with a smash, the smash is returned with a drop, and the drop is returned with a clear. The cycle is repeated. The order of shots for the first player is clear, drop, smash, clear, drop, smash, etc. For the second player, it is smash, clear, drop, smash, clear, drop, etc. In other words, partners smash the clear, drop-shot the smash, and clear the drop shot. This pattern is continued until one person misses, then it is started an gain.

1. Deep Singles Serves

Mark the court from the baseline forward in 2-foot increments. Take ten serves. If you serve the shuttle into the deepest section, give yourself 4 points. The next section in is worth 3 points, the next section 2 points, and the closest section is 1 point. A perfect score would be 40 points.

2. Low Doubles Serve

Mark the court in 1-foot increments from the service line back. Take ten serves. If you serve low (within 1 foot of the net) and to the closest area (short service line to 1 foot back), give yourself 4 points. The next area (1 foot to 2 feet from the service line) is worth 3, the next area (2 to 3 feet from the short service line) is worth 2 points, and the farthest area (3 to 4 feet from the service line) is worth 1. A perfect score would be 40 points.

3. Forehand and Backhand Clears

Mark the court with four 2-feet increments starting from the baseline. From a position in the backcourt, a partner will hit you ten shots to your forehand

and then ten to your backhand. Your scores will be 1, 2, 3, or 4 depending on which increment area you hit your high clear shot into. From the end line to 2 feet in is 4 points, from 2 to 4 feet in is 3 points, etc.

(Note: a more advanced player may be needed to "feed" the shuttle into the backcourt.)

4. Drop Shots

With the court marked in 2-foot increments

from the net, and you playing from near the midcourt, hit ten drop shots. The score is 4 if the shuttle lands within 2 feet of the net, 3 if it lands 2 to 4 feet from the net, 3 if it lands 2 feet inside the service line, and 4 if it lands 2 feet past the service line.

5. Smash

While standing midcourt, have a partner set you up with a short clear. Smash into the other court. You get 4 points if you hit the shuttle between the back

boundary line and the back doubles service court line, 3 points if you hit it from the back doubles court line to a point 4 feet forward of that point, 2 points if you hit it from the next closest 4-foot area, and 1 point if you hit it from the service line to 4 feet back.

Summary

1. Drills are essential to making rapid progress in any sport.
2. Concentrate on what you are doing.

APPENDIX A
The LAWS of Badminton

The Laws of Badminton. *As amended and adopted by the BWF May 2010. Historical Versions are also available. The Laws are a subset of the full BWF Handbook*, which also covers many aspects of competition.

Index to The Laws of Badminton

1. COURT
2. SHUTTLE
3. TESTING A SHUTTLE FOR SPEED
4. RACKET
5. EQUIPMENT COMPLIANCE
6. TOSS
7. SCORING
8. CHANGE OF ENDS
9. SERVICE
10. SINGLES
11. DOUBLES
12. SERVICE COURT ERRORS
13. FAULTS
14. LETS
15. SHUTTLE NOT IN PLAY
16. CONTINUOUS PLAY, MISCONDUCT, PENALTIES
17. OFFICIAL AND APPEALS

DEFINITIONS

- **Player:** Any person playing Badminton.
- **Match:** The basic contest in Badminton between opposing sides each of one or two players.
- **Singles:** A match where there is one player on each of the opposing sides.
- **Doubles:** A match where there are two players on each of the opposing sides.

- **Serving side:** The side having the right to serve.
- **Receiving side:** The side opposing the serving side.
- **Rally:** A sequence of one or more strokes starting with the service, until the shuttle ceases to be in play.
- **Stroke:** A movement of the player's racket with an intention to hit the shuttle.

The Laws of Badminton

1. COURT AND COURT EQUIPMENT

1.1. The court shall be a rectangle marked out with lines 40 mm wide as shown in Diagram A.

1.2. The lines marking out the court shall be easily distinguishable and preferably be coloured white or yellow.

1.3. All the lines shall form part of the area which they define.

1.4. The posts shall be 1.55 metres in height from the surface of the court and shall remain vertical when the net is strained as provided in Law 1.10.

1.5. The posts shall be placed on the doubles side lines as in Diagram A irrespective of whether singles or doubles is being played. The posts or its supports shall not extend into the court beyond the side lines.

1.6. The net shall be made of fine cord of dark colour and even thickness with a mesh of not less than 15 mm and not more than 20 mm.

1.7. The net shall be 760 mm in depth and at least 6.1 metres wide.

1.8. The top of the net shall be edged with a 75 mm white tape doubled over a cord or cable running through the tape. This tape shall rest upon the cord or cable.

1.9. The cord or cable shall be stretched firmly, flush with the top of the posts.

1.10. The top of the net from the surface of the court shall be 1.524 metres at the centre of the court and 1.55 metres over the side lines for doubles.

1.11 There shall be no gaps between the ends of the net and the posts. If necessary, the full depth of the net at the ends shall be tied to the posts.

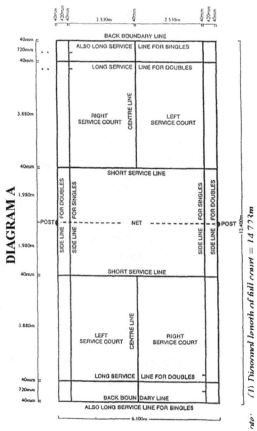

Note: (1) Diagonal length of full court = 14.723m
(2) Court as shown above can be used for both singles and doubles play
(3) ** Optional testing marks as shown in Diagram B.

2. **SHUTTLE**

2.1 The shuttle shall be made of natural and / or synthetic materials. From whatever material the shuttle is made, the flight characteristics generally shall be similar to those produced by a natural feathered shuttle with a cork base covered by a thin layer of leather.

2.2 Feathered Shuttle

2.2.1 The shuttle shall have 16 feathers fixed in the base.

2.2.2 The feathers shall have a uniform length between 62 mm to 70 mm when measured from the tip to the top of the base.

2.2.3 The tips of the feathers shall lie on a circle with a diameter from 58 mm to 68 mm.

2.2.4 The feathers shall be fastened firmly with thread or other suitable material.

2.2.5 The base shall be 25 mm to 28 mm in diameter and rounded on the bottom.

2.2.6 The shuttle shall weigh from 4.74 to 5.50 grams.

2.3 Non-Feathered Shuttle

2.3.1 The skirt, or simulation of feathers in synthetic materials, shall replace natural feathers.

2.3.2 The base shall be as described in Law 2.2.5.

2.3.3 Measurements and weight shall be as in Laws 2.2.2, 2.2.3 and 2.2.6. However, because of the difference in the specific gravity and other properties of synthetic materials in comparison with feathers, a variation of up to 10 per cent shall be acceptable.

2.4 Subject to there being no variation in the general design, speed and flight of the shuttle, modifications in the above specifications may be made with the approval of the Member Association concerned, in places where atmospheric conditions due to either altitude or climate make the standard shuttle unsuitable.

3. **TESTING A SHUTTLE FOR SPEED**

3.1 To test a shuttle, a player shall use a full underhand stroke which makes contact with the shuttle over the back boundary line. The shuttle shall be hit at an upward angle and in a direction parallel to the side lines.

3.2 A shuttle of correct speed will land not less than 530 mm and not more than 990 mm short of the other back boundary line as in Diagram B.

DIAGRAM B

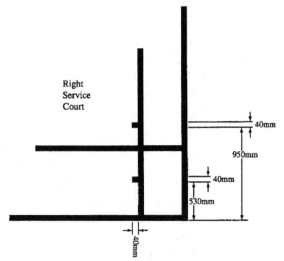

4. **RACKET**

4.1 The racket shall be a frame not exceeding 680 mm in overall length and 230 mm in overall width consisting of the main parts described in Laws 4.1.1 to 4.1.5 as illustrated in Diagram C.

4.1.1 The handle is the part of the racket intended to be gripped by a player.

4.1.2 The stringed area is the part of the racket with which it is intended that a player hits the shuttle.

4.1.3 The head bounds the stringed area.

4.1.4 The shaft connects the handle to the head (subject to Law 4.1.5).

4.1.5 The throat (if present) connects the shaft to the head.

DIAGRAM C

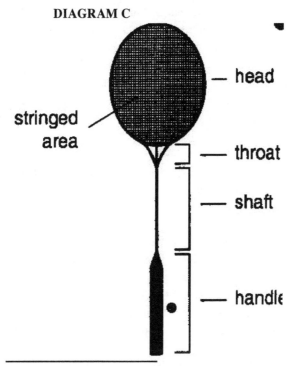

4.2 The stringed area:

4.2.1 shall be flat and consist of a pattern of crossed strings either alternately interlaced or bonded where they cross. The stringing pattern shall be generally uniform and, in particular, not less dense in the centre than in any other area; and

4.2.2 shall not exceed 280 mm in overall length and 220 mm in overall width. However, the strings may extend into an area which otherwise would be the throat, provided that:

4.2.2.1 the width of the extended stringed area does not exceed 35 mm; and

4.2.2.2 the overall length of the stringed area does not then exceed 330 mm.

4.3 The racket:

4.3.1 shall be free of attached objects and protrusions, other than those used solely and specifically to limit or prevent wear and tear, or vibration, or to distribute weight, or to secure the handle by cord to the player's hand, and which are reasonable in size and placement for such purposes; and

4.3.2 shall be free of any device that makes it possible for a player to change materially the shape of the racket.

5. **EQUIPMENT COMPLIANCE**

The International Badminton Federation shall rule on any question of whether any racket, shuttle or equipment or any prototype used in the playing of Badminton complies with the specifications. Such ruling may be undertaken on the Federation's initiative or on application by any party with a bona fide interest, including any player, technical official, equipment manufacturer or Member Association or member thereof.

6. TOSS

6.1 Before play commences, a toss shall be conducted and the side winning the toss shall exercise the choice in either Law 6.1.1 or 6.1.2:

6.1.1 to serve or receive first;

6.1.2 to start play at one end of the court or the other.

6.2 The side losing the toss shall then exercise the remaining choice.

7. SCORING SYSTEM

7.1 A match shall consist of the best of three games, unless otherwise arranged (Part II, Section 1B Appendix 2 and 3).

7.2 A game shall be won by the side which first scores 21 points, except as provided in Law 7.4 and 7.5.

7.3 The side winning a rally shall add a point to its score. A side shall win a rally, if the opposing side commits a "fault" or the shuttle ceases to be in play because it touches the surface of the court inside the opponent's court.

7.4 If the score becomes 20-all, the side which gains a two point lead first, shall win that game.

7.5 If the score becomes 29-all, the side scoring the 30th point shall win that game.

7.6 The side winning a game shall serve first in the next game.

8. CHANGE OF ENDS

8.1 Players shall change ends:

8.1.1 at the end of the first game;

8.1.2 at the end of the second game, if there is to be a third game; and

8.1.3 in the third game when a side first scores 11 points.

8.2 If the ends are not changed as indicated in Law 8.1, it shall be done so as soon as the mistake is discovered and when the shuttle is not in play. The existing score shall stand.

9. SERVICE

9.1 In a correct service:

9.1.1 neither side shall cause undue delay to the delivery of the service once the server and the receiver are ready for the service. On completion of the backward movement of server's racket head, any delay in the start of the service (Law 9.2), shall be considered to be an undue delay;

9.1.2 the server and the receiver shall stand within diagonally opposite service courts (Diagram A) without touching the boundary lines of these service courts;

9.1.3 some part of both feet of the server and the receiver shall remain in contact with the surface of the court in a stationary position from the start of the service (Law 9.2) until the service is delivered (Law 9.3);

9.1.4 the server's racket shall initially hit the base of the shuttle;

9.1.5 the whole shuttle shall be below the server's waist at the instant of being hit by the server's racket. The waist shall be considered to be an imaginary line round the body, level with the lowest part of the server's bottom rib;

9.1.6 the shaft of the server's racket at the instant of hitting the shuttle shall be pointing in a downward direction;

9.1.7 the movement of the server's racket shall continue forwards from the start of the service (Law 9.2) until the service is delivered (Law 9.3);

9.1.8 the flight of the shuttle shall be upwards from the server's racket to pass over the net so that, if not intercepted, it shall land in the receiver's service court (i.e. on or within the boundary lines); and

9.1.9 in attempting to serve, the server shall not miss the shuttle.

9.2 Once the players are ready for the service, the first forward movement of the server's racket head shall be the start of the service.

9.3 Once started (Law 9.2), the service is delivered when the shuttle is hit by the server's racket or, in attempting to serve, the server misses the shuttle.

9.4 The server shall not serve before the receiver is ready. However, the receiver shall be considered to have been ready if a return of the service is attempted.

9.5 In doubles, during the delivery of service (Law 9.2, 9.3), the partners may take up any positions within their respective courts, which do not unsight the opposing server or receiver.

10. **SINGLES**

10.1 Serving and receiving courts

10.1.1 The players shall serve from, and receive in, their respective right service courts when the server has not scored or has scored an even number of points in that game.

10.1.2 The players shall serve from, and receive in, their respective left service courts when the server has scored an odd number of points in that game.

10.2 Order of play and position on court.

In a rally, the shuttle may be hit by the server and the receiver alternately, from any position on that player's side of the net, until the shuttle ceases to be in play (Law 15).

10.3 Scoring and serving

10.3.1 If the server wins a rally (Law 7.3), the server shall score a point. The server shall then serve again from the alternate service court.

10.3.2 If the receiver wins a rally (Law 7.3), the receiver shall score a point. The receiver shall then become the new server.

11. **DOUBLES**

11.1 Serving and receiving courts

11.1.1 A player of the serving side shall serve from the right service court when the serving side has not scored or has scored an even number of points in that game.

11.1.2 A player of the serving side shall serve from the left service court when the serving side has scored an odd number of points in that game.

11.1.3 The player of the receiving side who served last shall stay in the same service court from where he served last. The reverse pattern shall apply to the receiver's partner.

11.1.4 The player of the receiving side standing in the diagonally opposite service court to the server shall be the receiver.

11.1.5 The players shall not change their respective service courts until they win a point when their side is serving.

11.1.6 Service in any turn of serving shall be delivered from the service court corresponding to the serving side's score, except as provided in Law 12.

11.2 Order of play and position on court

After the service is returned, in a rally, the shuttle may be hit by either player of the serving side and either player of the receiving side alternately, from any position on that player's side of the net, until the shuttle ceases to be in play (Law 15).

11.3 Scoring and serving

11.3.1 If the serving side wins a rally (Law 7.3), the serving side shall score a point. The server shall then serve again from the alternate service court.

11.3.2 If the receiving side wins a rally (Law 7.3), the receiving side shall score a point. The receiving side shall then become the new serving side.

11.4 Sequence of serving

In any game, the right to serve shall pass consecutively:

11.4.1 from the initial server who started the game from the right service court

11.4.2 to the partner of the initial receiver.

11.4.3 to the partner of the initial server

11.4.4 to the initial receiver,

11.4.5 to the initial server and so on.

11.5 No player shall serve or receive out of turn, or receive two consecutive services in the same game, except as provided in Law 12.

11.6 Either player of the winning side may serve first in the next game, and either player of the losing side may receive first in the next game.

12. **SERVICE COURT ERRORS**

12.1 A service court error has been made when a player:

12.1.1 has served or received out of turn; or

12.1.2 has served or received from the wrong service court;

12.2 If a service court error is discovered, the error shall be corrected and the existing score shall stand.

13. **FAULTS**

It shall be a "fault":

13.1 if a service is not correct (Law 9.1);

13.2 if, in service, the shuttle:

13.2.1 is caught on the net and remains suspended on its top;

13.2.2 after passing over the net, is caught in the net; or

13.2.3 is hit by the receiver's partner;

13.3 if in play, the shuttle:

13.3.1 lands outside the boundaries of the court (i.e. not on or within the boundary lines);

13.3.2 passes through or under the net;

13.3.3 fails to pass over the net;

13.3.4 touches the ceiling or side walls;

13.3.5 touches the person or dress of a player;

13.3.6 touches any other object or person outside the court;

(Where necessary on account of the structure of the building, the local badminton authority may, subject to the right of veto of its Member Association, make bye-laws dealing with cases in which a shuttle touches an obstruction).

13.3.7 is caught and held on the racket and then slung during the execution of a stroke;

13.3.8 is hit twice in succession by the same player. However, a shuttle hitting the head and the stringed area of the racket in one stroke shall not be a "fault";

13.3.9 is hit by a player and the player's partner successively; or

13.3.10 touches a player's racket and does not travel towards the opponent's court;

13.4 if, in play, a player:

13.4.1 touches the net or its supports with racket, person or dress;

13.4.2 invades an opponent's court over the net with racket or person except that the striker may follow the shuttle over the net with the racket in the course of a stroke after the initial point of contact with the shuttle is on the striker's side of the net;

13.4.3 invades an opponent's court under the net with racket or person such that an opponent is obstructed or distracted; or

13.4.4 obstructs an opponent, i.e. prevents an opponent from making a legal stroke where the shuttle is followed over the net;

13.4.5 deliberately distracts an opponent by any action such as shouting or making gestures;

13.5 if a player is guilty of flagrant, repeated or persistent offences under Law 16;

14. **LETS**

14.1 "Let" shall be called by the umpire, or by a player (if there is no umpire), to halt play.

14.2 It shall be a "let", if:

14.2.1 the server serves before the receiver is ready (Law 9.4);

14.2.2 during service, the receiver and the server are both faulted;

14.2.3 after the service is returned, the shuttle is:

14.2.3.1 caught on the net and remains suspended on its top, or

14.2.3.2 after passing over the net is caught in the net;

14.2.4 during play, the shuttle disintegrates and the base completely separates from the rest of the shuttle;

14.2.5 in the opinion of the umpire, play is disrupted or a player of the opposing side is distracted by a coach;

14.2.6 a line judge is unsighted and the umpire is unable to make a decision; or

14.2.7 any unforeseen or accidental situation has occurred.

14.3 When a "let" occurs, play since the last service shall not count and the player who served last shall serve again,.

15. SHUTTLE NOT IN PLAY

A shuttle is not in play when:

15.1 it strikes the net or post and starts to fall towards the surface of the court on the striker's side of the net;

15.2 it hits the surface of the court; or

15.3 a "fault" or a "let" has occurred.

16. CONTINUOUS PLAY, MISCONDUCT & PENALTIES

16.1 Play shall be continuous from the first service until the match is concluded, except as allowed in Laws 16.2 and 16.3.

16.2 Intervals:

16.2.1 not exceeding 60 seconds during each game when the leading score reaches 11 points; and

16.2.2 not exceeding 120 seconds between the first and second game, and between the second and third game shall be allowed in all matches.

(For a televised match, the Referee may decide before the match that intervals as in Law 16.2 are mandatory and of fixed duration).

16.3 Suspension of play

16.3.1 When necessitated by circumstances not within the control of the players, the umpire may suspend play for such a period as the umpire may consider necessary.

16.3.2 Under special circumstances the Referee may instruct the umpire to suspend play.

16.3.3 If play is suspended, the existing score shall stand and play shall be resumed from that point.

16.4 Delay in play

16.4.1 Under no circumstances shall play be delayed to enable a player to recover strength or wind or to receive advice.

16.4.2 The umpire shall be the sole judge of any delay in play.

16.5 Advice and leaving the court

16.5.1 Only when the shuttle is not in play (Law 15), shall a player be permitted to receive advice during a match.

16.5.2 No player shall leave the court during a match without the umpire's permission, except during the intervals as described in Law 16.2.

16.6 A player shall not:

16.6.1 deliberately cause delay in, or suspension of, play;

16.6.2 deliberately modify or damage the shuttle in order to change its speed or its flight;

16.6.3 behave in an offensive manner; or

16.6.4 be guilty of misconduct not otherwise covered by the Laws of Badminton.

16.7 Administration of breach

16.7.1 The umpire shall administer any breach of Law 16.4, 16.5 or 16.6 by:

16.7.1.1 issuing a warning to the offending side;

16.7.1.2 faulting the offending side, if previously warned. Two such faults by a side shall be considered to be a persistent offence; or

16.7.2 in cases of flagrant offence, persistent offences or breach of Law 16.2, the umpire shall fault the offending side and report the offending side immediately to the Referee, who shall have the power to disqualify the offending side from the match.

17. **OFFICIALS AND APPEALS**

17.1 The Referee shall be in overall charge of the tournament or event of which a match forms part.

17.2 The umpire, where appointed, shall be in charge of the match, the court and its immediate surrounds. The umpire shall report to the Referee.

17.3 The service judge shall call service faults made by the server should they occur (Law 9.1.2 to 9.1.8).

17.4 A line judge shall indicate whether a shuttle landed "in" or "out" on the line(s) assigned.

17.5 An official's decision shall be final on all points of fact for which that official is responsible except that if, in the opinion of the umpire, it is beyond reasonable doubt that a line judge has clearly made a wrong call, the umpire shall overrule the decision of the line judge.

17.6 An umpire shall:

17.6.1 uphold and enforce the Laws of Badminton and, especially, call a "fault" or a "let" should either occur;

17.6.2 give a decision on any appeal regarding a point of dispute, if made before the next service is delivered;

17.6.3 ensure players and spectators are kept informed of the progress of the match;

17.6.4 appoint or replace line judges or a service judge in consultation with the Referee;

17.6.5 where another court official is not appointed, arrange for that official's duties to be carried out;

17.6.6 where an appointed official is unsighted, carry out that official's duties or play a "let";

17.6.7 record and report to the Referee all matters relating to Law 16; and

17.6.8 refer to the Referee all unsatisfied appeals on questions of law only. (Such appeals must be made before the next service is delivered or, if at the end of the match, before the side that appeals has left the court).

The information here is presented as-is. My intention is for this to be as accurate as possible, but I can assume no responsibility for errors or omissions. This is the official publication of the BWF rendered as HTML. Please contact me with any corrections or updates and I will incorporate them into this presentation. Last revised: 16 March 2011 17:39.

For further information:
www.worldbadminton.com/rules) contact:
Stan Bischoff   stan@worldbadminton.com

Badminton Terms

Alley: The 1 1/2-foot-wide area on each side of the court that is used for doubles.

Around-the-Head Stroke: An overhead stroke used when hitting a forehand-like overhead stroke which is on the backhand side of the body.

Back Alley: The area between the doubles' long service line and the back baseline.

Back Court: Approximately the back third of the court. **Backhand: A** stroke made on the non-racket side of the body.

Base: *See* home base. Also the cork part of the shuttle in which the feathers are attached.

Baseline: The back boundary line of the **court. Bird:** Another name for shuttlecock or shuttle.

Block: A soft shot, used primarily against a smash, in which there is little or no backswing or follow-through.

Carry: Called when the shuttle stays on the racket during a stroke. It is legal if the racket follows the intended line of flight. Also called *throw*.

Centerline: The line parallel with the sidelines, separating the service courts.

Clear: A high shot that goes over your opponent's head and lands close to the backline. Also called *lob*.

Combination Doubles Formation: Where the partners play both up and back and side by side.

Crosscourt: A shot hit diagonally into the opposite court.

Dab: A blocking action for a shot. Also called *push*.

Double Hit: An illegal shot in which the racket contacts the shuttle twice in one swing.

Doubles Service Court: The short, wide area (13 feet x 10 feet) to which the server must serve.

Down-the-Line Shot A shot hit straight ahead—usually down the sideline. Dribble: *See* hairpin **drop.**

Drive: A hard-driven **stroke that clears the net but does not go high** enough for your opponent to **smash.**

Drive Serve: A hard serve **similar to the drive shot. It is used** most often in doubles games, with **a server serving from the right court to the** backhand side of a right-handed player.

Drop: A shot that just clears the net, then falls close to it. Face: The wide part of the racket—the part with the strings.

Fault: Any infraction of the rules. It results in the loss of serve or in a point for the server.

First Serve: A term used in doubles to indicate that the person serving is the first server of the inning.

Flick: A quick wrist action that speeds the flight of the shuttle.

Foot Fault: Called when the server's feet are out of the proper service court or when they leave the floor during a serve.

Forecourt: The area near the net—approximately between the net and the short service line.

Forehand: Any stroke made on the racket side of the body. Game **Point:** The point that ends the game.

Hairpin Drop Shot: A soft shot made from close to the net and low, just clearing the net, then dropping nearly straight down.

Halfcourt Shot: A low shot that lands at approximately midcourt. It is used most often in doubles against teams playing in an up-and-back alignment.

Hand In: The term used to indicate that the server retains the serve.

Hand Out or One Hand Down: The term used in doubles when one player has lost service.

Home Base: The position in the center of the court from which the player can best play any shot hit by the opponent.

IBF: The International Badminton Federation—the world governing body.

Inning: The period of time during which a singles player or a doubles team is serving.

fast, downward return, such as a smash, which should end the point.

Let: Called when play is stopped because of some outside interference. The point is then replayed.

Lob: *See* clear.

Long Serve: A high serve landing near the backline of the receiver. Love: A term sometimes used to indicate that the score is zero.

Match: A series of games. The winner must win two out of three games or three out of five to win the match.

Match Point: The point that, if won, will win the game.

Midcourt: The middle third of the court, between the net and the baseline.

Net Shot: A shot executed in the forecourt that barely clears the top of the net.

Offense: The team or player that is hitting downward returns or forcing the opponent to lift the shuttle in the return.

Overhead: The arm action used to hit a shuttle when it is above one's head.

Placement: Controlling where a shot will land. Good placement directs a shot to an area of the court from which the opponent will find it difficult to make an effective return.

Pronation: The inward rotation of the wrist and forearm used for all overhead forehand strokes that require power.

Put the Bird on the Floor: End the rally with a kill or a well-hit placement where the opponents cannot get a racket on the bird.

Racket: The implement used to hit the shuttle.

Racket Foot: The foot on the racket side of the body. It will be forward on underhand strokes.

Rally: A period of hitting the shuttle back and forth over the net—either during practice or during a game.

Ready Position: The balanced position that a player assumes to be ready to move in any direction. The weight is on the balls of the feet, knees are bent, and the torso leans forward.

Receiver: The player to whom the shuttle is served.

Round the **Head:** *See* around-the-head shot.

Rush the Serve: A tactic used mostly in doubles by the receiver to quickly attack a low serve.

Scissors: The changing of position of the feet taken during a shot so that

the hitter can get to the home-base area more quickly.

Second Serve: In doubles, the term indicates that one partner has lost the serve and the other partner is serving.

Server: The player who starts the play.

Set-Up: A shot that gives the opponent an easy chance to win the rally.

Setting: Making the choice as to how many more points to play when the score is tied one or two points before the game should be over—such as at 13 or 14 in a 15-point game.

Short Serve: A serve that clears the net low and lands just beyond the service line. It is used primarily in doubles play.

Shuttlecock or Shuttle: The feathered cork or plastic missile that is hit in the game of badminton.

Side By Side: A defensive formation used in doubles, in which each partner is responsible for one side of the court.

Side **Out:** When the individual or team loses the serve and the other team gets its chance to serve.

Smash: A hard overhead stroke hit sharply downward. It is the major attacking stroke in badminton.

Supination: The outward rotation of the wrist and forearm used for backhand strokes.

T: The intersection of the middle service and short service lines. **Underhand:** The stroke used when the shuttle is hit below shoulder level.

Unsight An illegal position taken by the server's partner so that the receiver cannot see the **serve as it is** hit.

Up and Back: An offensive formation used almost exclusively in mixed doubles, in which the front player is responsible for the forecourt and the partner for the backcourt.

CPSIA information can be obtained
at www.ICGtesting.com
Printed in the USA
LVHW012027291219
641942LV00042B/1562